Top Notes

T0360048

Ivan O'Mahoney's
Go Back to Where You Came From

Study notes for Common Module:
Texts and Human Experiences
2019–2023 HSC

Bruce Pattinson

A
FIVE SENSES
PUBLICATION

Five Senses Education Pty Ltd
2/195 Prospect Highway
Seven Hills 2147
New South Wales
Australia

Pattinson, Bruce
Top Notes – Go Back to Where You Came From
ISBN 978-1-76032-215-1

CONTENTS

TOP NOTES SERIES

This series has been created to assist HSC students of English in their understanding of set texts. Top Notes are easy to read, providing analysis of issues and discussion of important ideas contained in the texts.

Particular care has been taken to ensure that students are able to examine each text in the context of the module it has been allocated to.

Each text generally includes:

- Notes on the specific module
- Plot summary
- Character analysis
- Setting
- Thematic concerns
- Language studies
- Essay questions and a modelled response
- Other textual material
- Study practice questions
- Useful quotes

We have covered the areas we feel are important for students in their study of *Texts and Human Experiences* for their Common Module. I am sure you will find these Top Notes useful in your studies of English.

Bruce Pattinson
Series Editor

COMMON MODULE:
TEXTS AND HUMAN EXPERIENCES

*"It is quite possible—overwhelmingly probable, one might guess—
that we will always learn more about human life and personality
from novels than from scientific psychology"*

NOAM CHOMSKY

What is the Common Module?

The Common Module set for the 2019–23 HSC is *Texts and Human Experiences*. It is compulsory to study this topic as prescribed by NESA and it is common to all three English courses. Remember: you will be learning how texts reveal individual and collective human experiences. There are no right or wrong answers in this module – it is about how you see and interpret material and engage with it.

In the Common Module you will be analysing one prescribed text and a range of short texts that are related to the idea of human experiences. You will analyse texts not only to investigate the ideas they present about this area but also how they convey these ideas. This means you will be looking closely at the techniques a composer uses to represent his / her messages and shape meaning. You will also be looking at relationships between texts in regard to the experiences you explore. Overall, you will become an expert on texts and the human experience — that is, the different notions people have about human experience and the various ways composers manipulate techniques to communicate their ideas about it.

Specifically you will look at one set text from the following list.

- Doerr, Anthony, *All the Light We Cannot See*
- Lohrey, Amanda, *Vertigo*
- Orwell, George, *Nineteen Eighty-Four*
- Parrett, Favel, *Past the Shallows*
- Dobson, Rosemary 'Young Girl at a Window', 'Over the Hill', 'Summer's End', 'The Conversation', 'Cock Crow', 'Amy Caroline', 'Canberra Morning'
- Slessor, Kenneth 'Wild Grapes', 'Gulliver', 'Out of Time', 'Vesper-Song of the Reverend Samuel Marsden', 'William Street', 'Beach Burial'
- Harrison, Jane, *Rainbow's End*
- Miller, Arthur, *The Crucible*
- Shakespeare, William, *The Merchant of Venice*
- Winton, Tim, *The Boy Behind the Curtain* Chapters: 'Havoc: A Life in Accidents', 'Betsy', 'Twice on Sundays', 'The Wait and the Flow', 'In the Shadow of the Hospital', 'The Demon Shark', 'Barefoot in the Temple of Art'
- Yousafzai, Malala & Lamb, Christina, *I am Malala*
- Daldry, Stephen, *Billy Elliot*
- O'Mahoney, Ivan, *Go Back to Where You Came From –* Series 1, Episodes 1, 2 and 3 and *The Response*
- Walker, Lucy, *Waste Land*

NESA has mandated that students must study a related text as part of the common module, and that this should be part of their in-school assessment. However there is NO LONGER a requirement to write about a related text in the HSC examination itself.

WHAT DOES NESA REQUIRE FOR THE COMMON MODULE?

The NESA documentation of the Common Module: Texts and Human Experiences states that students:

- deepen their understanding of how texts represent individual and collective human experiences;

- examine how texts represent human qualities and emotions associated with, or arising from, these experiences;

- appreciate, explore, interpret, analyse and evaluate the ways language is used to shape these representations in a range of texts in a variety of forms, modes and media;

- explore how texts may give insight into the anomalies, paradoxes and inconsistencies in human behaviour and motivations, inviting the responder to see the world differently, to challenge assumptions, ignite new ideas or reflect personally;

- may also consider the role of storytelling throughout time to express and reflect particular lives and cultures;

- by responding to a range of texts, further develop skills and confidence using various literary devices, language concepts, modes and media to formulate a considered response to texts;

- study one prescribed text and a range of short texts that provide rich opportunities to further explore representations of human experiences illuminated in texts;

- make increasingly informed judgements about how aspects of these texts, for example, context, purpose, structure, stylistic and grammatical features, and form shape meaning;

- select one related text and draw from personal experience to make connections between themselves, the world of the text and their wider world;

- by responding and composing throughout the module, further develop a repertoire of skills in comprehending, interpreting and analysing complex texts;

- examine how different modes and media use visual, verbal and/or digital language elements;

- communicate ideas using figurative language to express universal themes and evaluative language to make informed judgements about texts;

- further develop skills in using metalanguage, correct grammar and syntax to analyse language and express a personal perspective about a text

If this is what is required by NESA, we need to examine the concept of human experience carefully so we can adequately respond in these ways. I would recommend that you read the complete document which is on the NESA web site and can be downloaded in Word or Adobe. Understanding this document is an important step in handling the textual material within the guidelines required — remember you are reading for a purpose and should make notes and highlight ideas as you read so that you can develop these ideas later.

UNDERSTANDING THE COMMON MODULE

What are Human Experiences?

The concept of Human Experiences is at the heart of the Common Module.

Human Experiences are experiences of individuals or a group of people (eg a family, society, or nation) in life. There are a very wide range of human experiences which include but go beyond this list:

- feelings or reactions (momentary or long term): love, hate, anger, joy, fear, disgust
- key milestones or stages: birth, childhood, adulthood, marriage, divorce, death
- culture, belonging and identity
- conformity and rebellion
- innocence and guilt, justice
- freedom and repression
- education, vocation, work, sport, leisure
- attraction to a person, idea, group or cause
- opposition to an idea, cause, political system
- religious faith or belief
- extreme events such as an earthquake, avalanche, tsuanami
- regular events such as walking, eating, singing, dancing, discussing ideas.

The word *experience* seems innately connected to the human condition and it is something we have each day whether a mundane experience that is repetitive, or something new and dramatic which offers challenges and rewards. Experiences can vary greatly in their impact on individuals, groups and countries. One example might be a war that is a negative experience for a whole population while we may experience the wonder of medicine with a new vaccine for a deadly disease that saves millions of people. We need to note that the module asks for 'experiences' ...we are a combination of different experiences and each has a varying impact. One person's problem is another's challenge depending on perspective, skill set, previous experience and ability.

Experiences are widespread and often shared: this is why people tell their stories and these shared experiences form part of our cultural heritage. These experiences often inform, warn and teach across entire cultural groups and many stories are shared across cultures.

DEFINING HUMAN EXPERIENCES

Now let's attempt to define what human experiences are and shape them into a more coherent and easily understood framework so we can begin our investigation at a basic level of understanding before moving into more complex analysis and looking at how the texts illuminate our understanding of the term.

Dictionary.com defines the term **experience** as:

noun

1. a particular instance of personally encountering or undergoing something:

2. the process or fact of personally observing, encountering, or undergoing something:

3. the observing, encountering, or undergoing of things generally as they occur in the course of time:
   to learn from experience; the range of human experience.

4. knowledge or practical wisdom gained from what one has observed, encountered, or undergone, e.g. *a man of experience.*

5. *Philosophy*. the totality of the cognitions given by perception; all that is perceived, understood, and remembered.

verb

(used with object), **experienced, experiencing.**

6. to have experience of; meet with; undergo; feel, e.g. *to experience nausea.*

7. to learn by experience.

idiom

8. **experience religion**, to undergo a spiritual conversion by which one gains or regains faith in God.

Obviously there are a number of definitions according to context, but all are applicable to our study in some shape or form, as the range of human experience is so vast. The search for 'new experience' has driven much of the development of people, groups, cultures and nations over past millennia. New experiences are always met with excitement and often trepidation as to what change they might bring.

Think historically about how people have reacted to change. It can cause great upheavals in society, with violent reactions while other changes brought through various experiences are welcomed and may change how people live and comprehend the world. Experiences affect us emotionally in many cases rather than logically and when we respond emotionally, behaviours become unpredictable. This causes the paradoxes, anomalies and inconsistencies mentioned in the rubric. If we were logical beings the world would be an easier place, but probably more boring.

These definitions all point to the fact that memory is the key to experience. The experience is stored in memory and drawn upon when the circumstances are repeated or closely mimicked so we can deal with them — hopefully better than on the initial experience.

Experiences can come in many ways and the synonyms listed below for experience help us to understand the concept even further. They assist in defining how an experience can arise:

Synonyms

actions

background

contacts

involvement

know-how

maturity

participation

patience

practice

reality

sense

skill

struggle

training

understanding

wisdom

acquaintances

actuality

caution

combat

doings

empiricism

evidence

existences

exposures

familiarity

intimacy

inwardness

judgment

observation

perspicacity

practicality

proofs

savoir-faire

seasonings

sophistication

strife

trials

worldliness

forebearance

http://www.thesaurus.com/browse/experience.?s=t

These synonyms show partly the vast array of words that our language has created around this concept, and also shows how important it is in the human psyche. We, as humans, want to experience. Now we will look at some examples of experiences and examine how they can have an impact. It is also important to remember that experiences do not have to be positive. You might experience a huge problem, a bereavement, a car accident, an unwelcome relationship or something totally bizarre that rocks your world. There can be a more opaque side to any experience that may need to be addressed.

The whole aim of this Common Module is to examine the text closely but also relate it to the concept of human experiences and decide how examining it in this way enables us to better understand both the text and the concept of humanity.

It is important that you unpack what each text you study shows you about human experiences and what ideas / themes arise from those experiences. Formulate your own ideas about the text.

Read the NESA Stage 6 document called *English Stage 6: Annotations of selected texts prescribed for the Higher School Certificate 2019-23* (see *www.educationstandards.nsw.edu.au*) for the set text you are studying. This document offers insights into the way each particular text should be examined by outlining key ideas and areas for clarification.

Human experiences and ways of experiencing vary due to individual circumstance and these experiences can change many things about individual lives, communities and the world. When we examine the concept of human experience in relation to a text, we need to examine the assumptions or biases we bring to it as well as how experiencing the text itself may change us and how we view things. The text may challenge and confront how we view the human experience or we may have preconceived ideas that make it more difficult for this to happen.

Students can also think about their own 'personal experience to make connections between themselves, the world of the text and their wider world.' Examining and enjoying any text is an experience in itself but it is what we take away from the text and apply that is the crucial aspect. That is not to say that every text will be enjoyed or offer a human experience that is significant either positively or negatively. Some texts may not personally engage you and that is fine. This is especially so when you begin to look for other related material that links to *Texts and Human Experiences*. We recommend that you find examples of texts that link but also personally appeal to you so that you can relate empathetically with them.

Individual Human Experiences

The idea of personal experiences is a popular and pervasive concept, especially in the literature of many cultures. Recording personal experiences as a means of sharing wisdom or more mundane daily tasks is part of human nature and we record and relate these experiences frequently. Experiences are recorded and relayed in many ways. We tell oral stories in both anecdotal and formal ways, we write, draw, sing and photograph our way into history (or not). Look at the proliferation of social media in this current century as people record their daily, even hourly, experiences for all to see. We record the most trivial details of our lives for likes and followers while the real world passes us by. Human experiences affect us on a daily basis and some experiences influence our lives and the way we live them.

Individuals seek out experiences in a variety of ways. Some seek more and more extreme experiences to test themselves against the world. Others limit their experiences. A lot of people prefer the familiar and don't actively seek new experiences. Individuals, it must be remembered, also see experiences in different ways and the same experience may have a very different impact on individuals. The one thing we can be certain about is that experiences are part of humanity and even the most limited of us have them. Many of these experiences also come from interaction with others and as noted we also like to share these experiences.

Experiences are what define us in many ways and are what makes us human.

We are going to look at four specific ways that experiences can influence us as people over the next few pages. These are physical, psychological, emotional and intellectual experiences and many experiences are a combination of these.

Physical Experience

The concept of a physical experience is tied into the human experience and part of the collective experience as well. Individuals seek physical experiences to test themselves against nature and other individuals often as part of trials and rituals, for example being integrated into a community. In modern times individuals have sought to test themselves with extreme sports and explorations into the harshest conditions and even space. Physical experiences can also change the way we see the world and others because of the chemical changes these experiences have on our bodies and mind. Physical experiences are often challenges and part of the experience is overcoming adversity. These physical challenges are often celebrated, as in the case of sports, but can also offer challenges if the experience is a negative one such as an accident or disease. Physical experiences are also often quite public and thus have permeated our societies in both their execution and how they are perceived. These physical experiences, even if experienced vicariously, have become popular across cultures and celebrated. Think of examples for yourself but most competitive sports offer examples.

Bruce Lee extends the concept of the physical experience into all aspects of life and that's what we will look at next in our analysis of human experiences –

'If you always put limits on everything you do, physical or anything else, it will spread into your work and into your life. There are no limits. There are only plateaus, and you must not stay there, you must go beyond them.'

Psychological Experience

The idea of a psychological experience is tied into many of the abstract ideas that people experience and can lead to a discussion of what is normal psychology. From the earliest times humans have attempted to alter their psychology through a number of experiences. On a simple level this can be a drug that changes the person's or group's perspective on reality. Examples of this might be alcohol or marijuana but cultural groups also use various substances to share group experiences. This can be seen in Native American cultures with *peyote*. In more modern times prescription drugs that are mood altering have been used to minimise the symptoms of psychiatric illnesses such as depression, and these mood altering drugs are common and legal. Others attempt to alter their psychology by seeing specialists in this area while others act out their condition leading to social and criminal issues. When discussing the human experience, psychology is a key issue and will form a part of most studies of experience. When taken too far this search for a new psychological experience can be harmful eg. an addiction.

Carl Jung, the famous psychologist, comments on the problems of addiction for human experiences, stating clearly that excess can be an issue:

"Every form of addiction is bad, no matter whether the narcotic be alcohol, morphine or idealism."

Emotional Experience

According to the psychologist, Robert Plutchik, there are eight basic emotions:

- **Fear** — feeling afraid.
- **Anger** — feeling angry. A stronger word for anger is rage.
- **Sadness** — feeling sad. Other words are sorrow, grief (a stronger feeling, for example when someone has died) or **depression** (feeling sad for a long time without any external cause). Some people think depression is a different emotion.
- **Joy** — feeling happy. Other words are happiness, gladness.
- **Disgust** — feeling something is wrong or nasty
- **Trust** — a positive emotion; admiration is stronger; acceptance is weaker
- **Anticipation** — in the sense of looking forward positively to something which is going to happen. **Expectation** is more neutral; **dread** is more negative.

https://simple.wikipedia.org/wiki/List_of_emotions

Emotions are the strongest drivers of human experience and form lasting aspects of any experience. Think about breaking up with someone you love and the emotions that drive behaviours in this situation. People have all sorts of extreme behaviours under the influence of emotions and these experiences are often the ones recorded and those which influence us most. Think about the role emotions play in our lives and the range of emotions from the list above. Consider how much emotions affect our life experiences, how they influence our decisions which decide our experiences and on a higher level consider how they affect the decisions which may seriously impact our experiences, such as politicians going to war.

Intellectual Experience

The concept of an intellectual experience is linked to decisions and experiences we have based on analysis and logic rather than the emotional choices referred to in the previous section. These intellectual experiences have changed the way we live and how we have seen our world. These experiences have affected the way we as humans have altered our world to suit our needs and lead to all the great advances in human society and thus experiences. Changes in our ideas, beliefs etc. alter the way we interact with the world and often these intellectual changes come at great cost.

Think of the time in Europe when the Church dominated and stopped scientific advances by calling them heresy/witchcraft. Open societies are more open to new ideas and this is what has hastened the pace of intellectual experiences as dominant ideologies fall away. Intellectual advances may not have the excitement that the other types produce but perhaps they have a more lasting impact on people, societies and the world in general. Ideas are powerful experiences and people hold beliefs strongly.

Immanuel Kant stated that:

> *"experience without theory is blind, but theory without experience is mere intellectual play."*

Consider this statement in the light of what we have learnt about human experiences. Are they a combination of many factors or can we isolate experiences into simple forms?

What exactly is a human experience?

The titular question reminds us of the old brainteaser: "If a tree falls in a forest and no one is around to hear it, does it make a sound?"

There are two classic responses to this. The more Platonically-minded would say the tree always makes a sound when it falls in the forest. We don't have to be there to hear it; we can imagine the sound of a tree falling in the forest, based on memory of such an event or on the recording of such an event. We know that sound is just vibrating air, and it's safe to say that air always vibrates in response to a tree falling, or a bear growling, or a cicada singing, whether we are there to hear it or not.

The second answer is a more post-structuralist response: the sound doesn't occur on its own; it needs a human ear to be heard. Therefore, if there is no human in the forest to hear the tree fall, then there is no sound. This automatically implies that "experience" of anything requires the presence of a human being, which means there is no such thing as an experience that *isn't* human.

Animal rights activists – or anyone with a beloved pet – would almost certainly reject this notion because it prioritises humans and relegates all other species to a lower class of being: an attitude that most would agree has gotten the human race into an awful lot of environmental trouble over the last 200 years of industrialisation.

In his article (*What is an Experience?*), my learned colleague Paul Hartley describes experience in its most basic form, as "the perception of something else" and "ultimately information about what we have perceived." But does this make it particularly human? Dogs and cats perceive things. Insects perceive things. You could even say that plants perceive things, such as the direction from which the sun is shining. Perception is the most basic of life's survival tools for all manner of flora and fauna.

In her brief but cogent disquisition on the subject (*What is Human?*), another of my learned colleagues, Nadine Hare, asserts that to be human is a social construct. Hartley builds on that notion by suggesting that culture affects experience when we start to share it, because "the words, associations, and priorities we attach to the shared experience define how we understand the world we live in."

Hare rightly points out that this world is increasingly dominated by consumerism, which has distorted what it means to be human by excluding all of the attributes and qualities that "make people people." Calling us consumers reduces our experiences to mere transactions. It defines human experience within the narrow confines of the purchase funnel and has little interest in anything that isn't a purchase driver.

Perhaps the field of commerce is where the experiential rubber most emphatically meets the road. Unlike mere perception, commerce is a uniquely human experience. It has mediated, automated, and dominated the human agenda to the point where we are defined by what we buy and little else. Commerce has invaded the non-profit spheres of government, health, and education, imposing its own priorities and principles on these institutions in the expectation that they will behave more like businesses. And even though business still strives to appeal to the so-called masses, it prioritises the pursuit of individual wealth, and in so doing, not only inhibits the desire for shared experience but unravels the social fabric historically woven by the democratic tradition.

As if in response, that social fabric is being re-woven by our networks. As Hare asserts, "humans both produce technology and are produced through technology." Experience is shared more now than it ever has been because the experiential platform – i.e., that very human invention called the internet – is in place to facilitate it like never before, and on a global scale.

This sharing capability reintroduces all of those things that "make people people" back into the conversation – whether commercial or political. What "makes people people" is messy, unpredictable, emotional, and complex. Most of what makes us human has no place in the experiential confines of the purchase funnel, and defies any of our attempts to place it there.

The challenge for us as a species is to embrace this new capacity for sharing to keep the agendas of our hegemonic institutions – whether commercial or political – from defining what makes an experience human. A post-consumer business strategy might be one that, as Hare hopes, will "expand our view of people to include the complex and dynamic social, cultural, gendered, spiritual and racialised beings that they are." Maybe then will our shared human experience truly become, as Hartley asserts, the glue that holds us all together as human beings.

Will Novosedlik
MISC magazine

https://miscmagazine.com/what-is-a-human-experience/

This article appeared in the September 2014 edition of MISC magazine. Can you relate to what the article says about human experiences? Do human experiences depend on perception? Does the experience of anything require the presence of a human as experiencer (para 3)? Can the ideas of experience be extended to include perception by plants or animals? Hartley's idea is that "shared human experience" is "the glue that holds us all together as human beings". Is this an oversimplification?

The Impact of Human Experiences

Human experiences have impacts on many levels. On an individual level, we can have changes in our assumptions about the world and people around us; we can ingest new ideas and have these open new vistas of productivity and performance. We can also reflect and build on these experiences to ensure that they are even more meaningful to our lives. Behaviours towards others and the way we respond to the world can manifest themselves in new and different responses. An example might be that through adverse experiences we can build resilience so that the next negative experience isn't as traumatic and we accept it for what it is. Experiences also teach us new behaviours on a very physical level — if you burn yourself once on a flame you learn not to do it again (hopefully).

The impact of human experiences can also be shared in groups and societies. Firstly, let's examine some group dynamics that can be affected by human experiences. Groups share experiences and adapt and develop behaviours that impact on the group as a whole. Think about the notorious 'bonding' sessions sporting teams have that unite them in a common goal. Think about the behaviours of various gangs in our society. We see plenty of examples of this on American television where gangs based on ethnicity and social groupings form specific sets of behaviours that impact on how they interact with each other and the world. These groupings carry assumptions about how they see the world and respond to it. For example, they may have generally negative reactions to law enforcement and this is ingrained into their codes of behaviour. They are suspicious of the world and the people in it — dividing them up into threats, the law and victims. These behaviours are often reinforced by group experiences such as the initiation rituals which are integral to membership.

Often the impact of these behaviours is to perpetuate stereotypes that then categorise the individuals within these groups. The graphic I have included here shows a stereotypical gang member with the suspicious gaze, ubiquitous hoody and scruffy look. These stereotypes reject new ideas and maintain assumptions about the world, often to the detriment of their members. The experiences they have reinforce their own stereotypical way of viewing anything outside the safety of the group and the cycle continues. Of course, other groups have more positive impacts and see the world as a  very different place and their experiences are designed to be positive interactions. Think about groups such as Rotary who are constructive in the community. Other groups have specialty interests such as Animal Welfare, Surf Lifesaving and charities.

Normal social interactions impact groups and individuals, but it takes a major event to alter the behaviours of whole societies, especially so in the modern world where societies are large in scale. Earlier in human history smaller experiences could alter the behaviour of societies as they were insignificant in size compared to modern ones. We often fail to remember that many of these ancient societies' behaviours were impacted by superstition, religions and cultural habituation. The modern society as we know it is only a recent phenomenon. Just a few hundred years ago with church rule people were forced to think in a specific

way and punished for not adhering to a theological culture. Think of the Spanish Inquisition, the imprisonment of Galileo and other such restrictions on freedom of thought; scientific breakthroughs were hidden or declared witchcraft. Even recently the world has seen societies kept repressed by failed ideologies. The brutality of such regimes has left deep scars on the social psyche of nations as they try to recover. This has had an impact on the human experiences of whole populations, and societies respond accordingly.

One example might be at the conclusion of the Communist regime in East Germany when the Berlin Wall was destroyed as a visual symbol of the new-found freedom of a whole population of people who had been repressed for decades by a brutal and ever-present regime. Many citizens who had grown up in this system, where you could 'disappear' without trial or real evidence, found the idea that you could express yourself incredible. Many of the

East Germans couldn't believe that this freedom was real and that the Stasi (the secret police) were gone.

Other experiences can affect societies in extreme ways. Think about wars and the impact they have on civilian populations.

Climatic events such as earthquakes change the way that people behave and respond to situations. Catastrophic flooding occurred in the US city of New Orleans in 2005. The US President's response to help was not immediate and the national administration was severely criticised for lack of effective action.

Societies also respond to perceived problems such as pollution. In 1989 the oil tanker Exxon Valdez ran aground in Prince William Sound, Alaska with disastrous results. The effects of this event are still being experienced thirty years later.

Societies can be divided, as we saw with the election of Donald Trump in the United States of America and the reaction of the Political Left.

The impact of human experiences on societies can be quite dramatic, as we have seen, while other experiences (such as an election) can go by without a murmur from societies, no matter who wins. As a last thought before we move on you should also consider the impact of the media on societies in the modern world, and how they influence individuals, societies and the development of ideas.

Problems With Human Behaviour

So far, we have discussed the impact of human experiences on behaviour. Now we can begin to develop some more complex judgements and understandings about the impact of those experiences on human behaviours. In simplistic terms it could be assessed as:

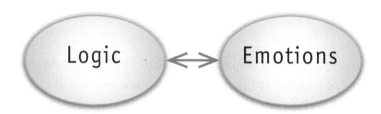

These two opposites on the continuum certainly shape the manner in which we see incidents and how they affect the experience. For instance, if someone you love has no interest in you, it creates a very different reaction to someone you don't care about having no interest in you. It is generally agreed that humans respond more strongly with emotion than they do with logic. Often, it is only through time and reflection that we can understand how an experience has changed and/or altered the manner in which we see a situation or individual.

The Role of Storytelling in Human Experiences

Storytelling has been part of the human experience since 'people' began communicating and it is a method used to convey information and experience as well as be entertaining. Earliest myths were all oral and then people began to write down stories so they weren't lost in time. From this, various theories have developed around storytelling and one is the 'monomyth', which is a template across cultures for storytelling. Let's have a look at this below.

'In narratology and comparative mythology, the monomyth, or the hero's journey, is the common template of a broad category of tales that involve a hero who goes on an adventure, and in a decisive crisis wins a victory, and then comes home changed or transformed.

The concept was introduced in *The Hero with a Thousand Faces* (1949) by Joseph Campbell, who described the basic narrative pattern as follows:

> "A hero ventures forth from the world of common day into a region of supernatural wonder: fabulous forces are there encountered and a decisive victory is won: the hero comes back from this mysterious adventure with the power to bestow boons on his fellow man."

Campbell and other scholars, such as Erich Neumann, describe narratives of Gautama Buddha, Moses, and Christ in terms of the monomyth. Critics argue that the concept is too broad or general to be of much use in comparative mythology. Others say that the hero's journey is only a part of the monomyth; the other part is a sort of different form, or colour, of the hero's journey.

https://en.wikipedia.org/wiki/Hero%27s_journey

Storytelling in History and its Purpose in Human Experience

Storytelling in oral form was accompanied by some theatrics to make the stories as entertaining as possible. Many of the early narratives were based upon religious ceremonies and stories of the creation of the earth and people(s). As time moved on, these stories were accompanied by dance, music and/or theatre and often were part of lengthy rituals, often taking days. These stories were designed to bring meaning to people's lives by explaining their own existence and the purpose/meaning of life in a time when life expectancy was short and entertainment was scarce. Of course stories were also recorded as these experiences were significant to all people and these stories run across all cultures. Before writing, stories were recorded in pictures such as cave art, in tattoo designs on skin and in designs such as rock piles and the giant carved heads of Easter Island.

Writing changed the manner in which stories were told and many of the old oral traditions were lost, barely being kept alive by specialists. Stories began to travel across cultural and national boundaries on whatever surface could be created. Papyrus, bones, pottery, skins, paper and in more modern times film, video and digital storage have changed, over time, the way in which stories of human experience have been told and shared. Content evolved from myth, fable and legend to history, personal narratives and commentary. Modern narrative form often has an educational or didactic element and can drift into propaganda. Stories of self-revelation can be instructive and give audiences the opportunity to apply learning to individual lives, whereas historically narrative was used in this way for societies and groups as a whole. In recent times narratives have become interactive and audiences can choose how the narrative unfolds.

Whatever form the story takes we all have a seemingly innate need for narratives to make sense of our lives. They either confirm our world view or alter our world view depending on the experience they convey and the experiences that we bring to the narrative. We need to remember that narratives are important to human experience and have been significant since the beginning of time.

The Text as an Experience

The concept of the text as an experience is one area to consider as we look at *Texts and Human Experiences*. Reading or viewing the text is an experience in itself and when we do this we bring our own history (experiences) to the text and this helps shape our understanding.

Think about the personal perspective that you bring to a text. What are some of your experiences that might influence how you read a particular text? Some texts, especially personal narratives of trial and tribulation or loss, can be confronting to some audiences and bring back strong opinions or emotions. Many texts attempt to do this as they convey a particular point of view about the world.

Does what you bring to the text affect what you learn from that text? We also need to delve into how the narrative experience is conveyed and how this in turn impacts upon the manner in which the story is received by audiences across different cultures. For example, Western films where heroes fight Islamic terrorism may well be viewed very differently by audiences in Western democracies and Islamic countries. Even seemingly innocuous narratives like the movie 'The Red Pill' which is about men's rights and created by a woman, has caused a polarisation of views wherever it has been shown. Strong personal experiences and viewpoints certainly bring their own understandings to texts.

Questions for Texts and Human Experiences

- Define the module in your own words.
- How are people connected by shared experiences?
- How might physical experience(s) change the way you respond to the world?
- How do you think a person's context and prior experiences shape how they perceive the world?
- Are experiences unique or do prior experiences have an impact on a current experience and way of seeing life?
- What is positive about human experiences?
- Discuss what is negative about human experiences.
- To what extent does experience shape the way we see other people and/or groups?
- Is an individual's culture part of their experience or is it something else?
- Is it possible not to have any meaningful experiences at all?
- Why do people tell stories?
- What do you think you might learn from a narrative?

STUDYING A DOCUMENTARY

A documentary according to dictionary.com is:

> a television show or film based on recreating an actual event, life story, era etc that purports to be factually accurate and contains no fictional content.

The documentary form has the concept of informing the audience of a 'real life' situation but you will note that the word 'purports' comes into the definition above. A documentary inherently has biases based on the beliefs of the producer/director even if they don't intentionally set out to project one particular point of view. The documentary deals with fact and are based in real life situations but at the core of a documentary is the need to touch the audience and call them to action in so much as it wants to inspire inner or social change. A documentary might/should inspire change and this is where the different techniques involved in making a documentary come into play.

A documentary will have an initial script that has to be adaptable as when you film real life situations flexibility is the key to enabling the audience to experience what the subject(s) are experiencing. This experience may/should evolve as the filming occurs. The subject that is the focus of the documentary concentrates on and in the early stages of documentaries they weren't even focused on being entertaining, just informative. While this has obviously changed over the past few decades and now we expect the form to be entertaining the focus must still be on the subject.

There is no specific formal structure or formulae for composing a documentary and they are all structured very differently, often depending on the subject. For example if they are about a person the footage will be focused on that individual but if it is a more amorphous subject such as climate change the challenges are very different for the producers. Documentaries can call on a variety of people and techniques to make their case. These include;

- Experts such as professors, politicians, billionaires, etc. depending on the subject
- Statistics
- Interviews
- On location shots
- Commentary i.e. voiceover
- Anecdotes, stories
- Graphs and charts
- Recounts and descriptions
- Dramatisations
- Use of colour, black and white, animation
- Montages
- Music, silences, sound
- Panel discussions with / without an audience

These are a few examples but you also need to consider the style of the documentary. For example older style classical documentaries are very rigidly chronological, factual and focused on dramatised realism. This has morphed into a more docu-drama style over the years and now audiences expect entertainment with their information. However, most documentaries still require extensive research so that the content is factual and verifiable. Even in documentaries such as *Go Back to Where You Came From* which is people based, to make a point the interactions have been researched, found and the content made accessible to the audience.

What the research does is ensure that the audience gets to see the heart of the issue, the part that is engaging, interesting and ultimately unique to that subject. A good documentary establishes a 'hook' to keep you interested, then presents the core assertion of the subject, arouses curiosity in the audience and gives hope of some change of action or ideas. Much like a fiction text, a documentary may also have a strong narrative, a protagonist, characters and a conclusion. You can use some of the ideas and knowledge, especially techniques, from your knowledge of fiction, just be alert to the subtle differences in the genres. In the documentary you can also have a backstory, points of view and some conflict which engenders emotions. It is the emotional engagement with the subject that creates empathy with the audience. We will examine how this is done by *Go Back to Where You Came From* later in this guide.

IVAN O'MAHONEY

Ivan O'Mahoney is an Australian producer and director who has been involved in a number of programs including *Great Southern Land*, *The Boys from Baghdad High*, *Borderland* and *How to Plan a Revolution*. He has degrees in international law and journalism, has been a litigation lawyer and a peacekeeper in Bosnia.

O'Mahoney has won numerous awards for his writing, direction and production with the majority of his work being about human rights issues. The series *Go Back to Where You Came From* won him awards from the AFI and even a Logie. He also won an Australian Directors Gold Award for Best Documentary in a Documentary Series.

O'Mahoney has said the series is 'a kind of blend between reality TV and an observational documentary.' In an interview with Graeme Blundell in *The Australian* newspaper he argues the neutrality of the series,

"Even those of the six who didn't change their positions came to appreciate that the discussion is not as simple as they had always thought," O'Mahoney says. "I don't want viewers to think that we want to manipulate them into being extremely welcoming of asylum-seekers or that we have a position that they are all bad and unwelcome."

As he suggests, "if the one thing the series achieves is to make people realise there is a more complex discussion to be had, it will have done its job. But it won't be easy."

http://www.theaustralian.com.au/arts/reality-show-participants-walk-a-mile-in-the-shoes-of-asylum-seekers/story-e6frg8n6-1226076364978

PLOT SUMMARY

Episode One

We begin our journey introducing the topic and the six Australians chosen for their 'strong views' on refugees. They are:

- **Raye** (63) a retired social worker who lives in the Adelaide Hills near a detention centre.

- **Roderick** (29) a liberal political aspirant from Brisbane who doesn't want to appear a 'leftie'

- **Raquel** (21) is unemployed and lives in Sydney's west, a self-admitted racist who left school at 14.

- **Darren** (42) a businessman from Adelaide, married to a Taiwanese wife with two children.

- **Gleny** (39) a musician and teacher from Newcastle who thinks we can take more refugees.

- **Adam** (26) a Cronulla lifeguard who was raised in the 'Shire' (Sutherland Shire of Sydney) and thinks refugees are 'criminals'.

All this is supervised by Dr David Corlett a Melbourne academic and refugee expert who provides information about refugees. The six Aussies are to live the life of a refugee for a month and see the reality behind the concept of what a refugee goes through. They are initially brought together at the former Defence Fortress in Sydney and then taken to their first experiences. It is a 'social experiment' which begins by them being stripped of their identities. We see their apprehension, especially as a few of them are not experienced travellers or worldly.

Throughout the episodes we learn more about each of the characters and their views. Each character develops a television persona and we need to remember that there is bias in the original concept and in what sections are edited for the show. It is designed to create empathy for the refugees and develop sympathy from the audience.

Raye, Raquel and Roderick are sent to Albury to live with an African family while the other three go to Liverpool to live with a group of Iraqi men. It is a journey in reverse for them as they begin by living with these families and learning their stories. In Liverpool we learn about the Iraqi war and how the men had to escape oppression. Think about why the man who interpreted for the Americans wanted his face scrambled on camera. The reality is different than the expected as we learn why the men had to surrender their documents and the life back home where death was a reality. On a trip to the local pool we learn of the different opinions between Gleny and Darren. At the pool we learn one of the Iraqi men is scared of water and we can imagine how hard the boat trip must have been. The man has post-traumatic stress disorder and the shock of what happens to these people is reinforced by a visit to Villawood Detention Centre.

Some of the stories from the detainees have shocked the group and they have a series of 'reality checks' through this experience. The final day of the visit has assured the three visitors that each of the refugees is a real person and that some are unconvinced the boat method is best. This new experience has challenged their assumptions about refugees and their circumstances.

In Albury the others go to live with the Masudi family, African refugees who have begun to forge a new life after fleeing Burundi and The Congo. The couple met in Kenya where they had fled from their respective countries. Even in the refugee camp they were robbed of food by locals and the conditions were poor. They had no money and experienced ill health. Maisara even wanted to suicide when she lost her baby her hopes of a better life were dimished. We learn later that her sisters were raped and one contracted AIDS and that many relatives were still there or dead. Her story deeply affects the two women but Raquel still, at the end of the visit, thinks the family is nice but still doesn't like all Africans. Bahati also tells of his incarceration and torture because of his political beliefs in Burundi. Maisara wants to be reunited with her family who have been in a refugee camp in Kenya for four years.

After this visit the group are all reunited in Darwin for an experience on a boat. They leave from Darwin and experience a journey on a makeshift boat with flooding in the bilge and then smoke. It is, of course, a set-up by the television producer but it is a real experience for them and it does create conflict and tension. We learn that the boat makes it a hard journey and we learn only two per cent of refugees come by boat. It is cramped and uncomfortable, especially for Raquel who becomes sea sick. A boat such as this normally carries fifty people and we see how this might cause problems.

Eventually the Coast Guard comes along and they are 'rescued' where they learn the truth about their predicament. On board the Coast Guard boat they learn the truth of their experience and recount the emotions they felt. Darren feels it is 'irresponsible' to put your family on a boat and argues that they are being forced to feel 'empathy' by the media. He doesn't want to be filmed any more. In the next episode they are told they are heading to a new destination overseas. We learn they are to go to Malaysia.

This physical experience takes on new meaning for them as it is real. Intriguingly Darren doesn't change his ideas and attitudes significantly and is quite firm in his opinions. Attitudes and perspectives can firm depending on the context of the experience and the initial views of the individual. Remember too, this occurs in a collective experience, so often outcomes are dependent on what an individual brings to that collective experience.

Questions for Episode One

1. Clearly delineate the views on refugees for each of the characters. At this early stage which individual do you like best and why?

2. Think about your views on refugees prior to watching this episode. Have they changed? Why/why not?

3. What do we learn about people's experiences in Iraq?

4. What do we discover about the complexity of life experiences in Africa, especially in Burundi or Angola?

5. Do you think the experiences the participants have in these initial exchanges alters their views? Explain fully with reference to the text.

6. Summarise what happens on the boat trip. Examine the reaction of each of the individuals to this group experience and think about the inconsistencies exposed in their thinking.

7. Why do you think the producers staged this experience? What do we learn about human behaviour from this experience?

8. Discuss ONE discovery made by one of the participants and use a quote to support your ideas.

9. What techniques are used by the makers of the documentary to influence the audience? Is the result in favour or against a particular point of view concerning refugees? Do they offer any alternate views?

10. Which participant makes the most interesting television and why? What have you discovered about them? Have you discovered anything yourself from this first episode?

Episode Two

This episode begins by recapping on the six people who are part of the experiment and on what happened to them and their views last episode. Then we get a précis of what is going to happen this week. We begin on a plane heading to Malaysia and learn Rod and Raquel have never travelled before but Raquel is determined to dress how she wants to despite it being a Muslim country. They travel through Kuala Lumpur and begin to assess the country. Malaysia is a 'staging post' where refugees live in 'limbo' where they are illegal and have few protections against arrest and detention. They are then told they are to live with a group of Burmese Chin, a persecuted minority.

The leader of the Chin group is Kennedy and he explains they fled from murder, rape and forced labour. Fifty people live in the flat and can't leave because of fear of arrest. It is crowded and lacks basic facilities including sanitation. Basic services are denied to them and the Australians are shocked at how they live and say it's 'primitive' but are impressed by the spirit of the children and how they adapt to their poor circumstances. Gleny thinks it is like a self-created 'detention centre'. Raquel complains about the children who are noisy into the night and the conditions at this stage the various experiences haven't changed her views but she now has a depth of experience that she hasn't had before and a wider perspective on which to evaluate her ideas.

The next morning they are awakened by the street noise and call to prayer before the men head off to work with their hosts. They are working illegally for food by clearing land. They do not get paid for the work but prefer this to construction where the chance of arrest is very high. The women attend a makeshift school with the children where over one hundred children are taught in four rooms. They are short on teachers so they have to teach English. They give it a go and Gleny is very successful as she is a more experienced teacher. It is depressing to think that these children will never have access to higher education. The men struggle with the work and Adam realises how easy life is in Australia. The experience has shown them how hard life is for the children especially and Raye becomes quite attached. It is interesting here that the experience is becoming more emotional and this is a powerful motivating force in changing ideas and offering new perspectives.

On completion of this visit after a week they are going to go on a border patrol and raid. In the helicopter they see the staging points and how the illegals hide in the mangroves. The officials say it is hard to catch the people smugglers and there has been no successful prosecution of people smugglers. That night the six travel on a raid to a construction site and watch how the illegals are caught and detained. They all have different views on this but the raid and its build-up make for good television rather than making any real point or impact. Over one hundred immigration officers, 'some armed' go on the raid. Illegals can be arrested, caned, detained and deported so it is quite dramatic for them and we see them try to escape and looked stunned when caught.

At the site men, women and children, including babies, are gathered up by the officers and taken away. The conditions they are living in are cramped, unhygienic and during the raid we see exactly what they have to live in. Raquel thinks it's 'exciting' and 'good' that they are arrested. Raye thinks it's 'sad' and states they, in here opinion, 'are not criminal'. The raid is 'full on' according to Darren and listen for the music which makes it more dramatic and certain points. Also think about the use of close ups, baby shots and mood music to engender sympathy for their plight. During the raid over one hundred people are caught and trucked away.

The six Australians review the raid and Gleny is 'deeply affected' while Raye wanted to 'stop it' but Raquel disagrees. Darren still wouldn't put his family on a boat in the same circumstances but Adam would. After this they are told they are heading to places many refugees go. Adam, Darren and Gleny are going to Jordan while the others are heading to Kenya and the refugee camps. Jordan is where Iraqi refugees flee to while in Kenya it is one of the biggest refugee camps in Africa. To get there they need an escort as the countryside is so dangerous. The driver says it's 'not like the Ivory Coast'. They are taken to a collection point for new refugees in the camp and are processed as if they are real refugees. They are in Kakuma camp ('nowhere') where eighty-four thousand refugees live.

They are placed in a communal hut where they must stay for a few days until they are permanently housed. The Australians' 'comfort zone' has been well and truly broken as they encounter the camp conditions and Raquel is very stressed because of the poor conditions and food. Raye and Raquel go to the toilets together but they are pits so Raquel refuses to go and is in tears. We end with a few scenes from the next episode and shots of Jordan and Iraq, Kenya and the Congo.

This episode is instructive in our study of human experiences because of the diversity of opinion and perspective stemming from the same collective experiences. The personal reflections are intriguing as are the manipulative techniques the producers use to get an emotional response from the participants. Can you see any pre-conceived bias in the production?

Questions for Episode Two

1. What is their initial impression of Malaysia? What view of the country does ONE participant give? Is this realistic or influenced because of pre-conceived ideas?

2. Describe the conditions the Chin live in. What made them leave Burma? What impact do you think their life experiences have had on these people?

3. What are the penalties for illegals in Malaysia? Why do you think the Malaysian government would have penalties such as this?

4. Describe how we see hope in the Chin people despite their many negative experiences.

5. How does Australia support the Malaysian government in the fight against illegals? How effective is this assistance?

6. Describe the build-up to the raid. Why might the producers / director include this in the episode?

7.   Analyse the differing views of the raid. What did each of the six Australians learn from their experience, if anything?

8.   How did you, as a viewer, feel about the raid on the construction site?

9.   Discuss how the camp in Kenya is framed by the director/cinematographer to create impact with the audience.

10. How do conditions in the camp impact on the three Australians? Is it a fair experience to give them?

Episode Three

We get the same recap of participants and events that occurred previously but also a preview of the nights viewing with quick shots and voice-over to make it more dramatic. In Africa they queue for food in a line of about ten thousand and are 'intimidated' by all the black faces. It takes an hour and a half to get food in the queue and then they get a paltry amount of food for two weeks but it doesn't seem much. The three Aussie are moved because of 'safety concerns' as the place is quite violent. They are to be moved to the more permanent camp.

Over in Oman, Jordan they join half a million refugees from the Iraqi war and firstly they visit a 'Médecins sans Frontières* hospital to see bomb victims and discover what they can about the situation. They are invited to a social day where they see the patients relax from some of the distress they are suffering. This experience is an emotive one because of the suffering they see

*Médecins sans Frontières...*Doctors without borders*

and the experiences of the injured and those working to assist them in difficult circumstances.

The scene then cuts back to Kenya where the three Aussies find the relatives of the Masudi family they lived with back in Albury. The twenty-five square kilometre camp is home to Bahati's brother and Maisara's sister. They are welcomed in their home and show a video message from Australia and bring news from the family which pleases them.

It is an emotional meeting because of its bittersweet nature. One part of the family is safe while the other lives in the camp. Bahati's brother, Deo, was tortured and his first family disappeared and admits life here is a struggle. They have no future, especially for the children, as their possibilities are limited. It is hard because they feel they are not seen with the 'heart'. This scene in the episode is emotive and framed so that the audience participates in the experience, albeit vicariously. It is emotive because of the familial circumstances and the personal contact the participants had with the Australian element of the family.

The scene then changes to Jordan where the three meet Wasmi's mother. She is being cared for by Rashid, Wasmi's brother who has come from America. The grandmother explains why he had to leave her behind as it was unsafe. She is sick and wants to come to Australia but her paperwork has been in limbo for over a year. The experience here involves ordinary people in extraordinary circumstances and this draws the audience into the experience i.e. it could be us.

Back in Kakuma the Australians take part in everyday life and we learn that Raquel has made a 'big shift' in what she thinks about the refugee situation. She has realised that she is 'spoilt' back in Australia. Here she has changed her ideas and reflected on her own circumstances and this is to her credit. The assumptions she had have altered as they have been challenged by what she has seen and experienced. Note here too that the method of 'storytelling' by the director is also influencing our experience and attempting to challenge how we see the refugee situation.

In Jordan, Rashid Skype's his family back in America and it is a happy moment. They share food and depart the small rooms that she lives in. After twenty days in the 'experiment' Adam recognises they have 'nothing' and no permanent solution in Jordan and can understand why they get on a boat while Darren says he has certainly been affected. It is an emotional time for all the participants. Then they are told they can choose to go to Iraq to see where they came from. They will be under the protection of the U.S. army in Baghdad.

Back in Kenya they are invited to go to the Congo where they will be under UN protection. Raquel chooses not to go and her farewell shows her philosophical change and newfound view of 'black' people.

Raye says her ideas have changed and she has a 'broader' picture of what being a refugee is. She now thinks she would 'do anything' to give her family a better life and would get on a boat and take a 'risk' for 'freedom'. We then change scenes to Kuwait where Darren, Adam and Gleny are geared up for the flight to Baghdad in a U.S Army Hercules. In Baghdad they stay in U.S Army headquarters in Saddam's old palace where they spend the night.

In Goma Congo they realise that security is big business and the war there is the biggest since World War Two. The Congo has seventy million people and we learn rape is a weapon of war and over a thousand women a day are raped. The makeshift camps on the edge of the city get food for fifteen days of the month and it is a struggle. To get firewood in the hills they risk rape so they have a soap machine to make money. The Aussies donate money to help fix it and they have a celebration where they sing 'There'll be no more rape' as the machine will be fixed. Rod thinks whoever can solve the conflict issue will win Nobel Peace Prize as it's so complicated. Note here how the director includes moments of positivity and hope to alleviate some of the tension which is great storytelling technique. While this is a documentary he is really telling a story.

In Baghdad, Gleny, Adam and Darren head out in an armoured car into city where they get a taste of the violence and tension in the streets. A one point the traffic stops and it makes everyone nervous as the convoy is 'vulnerable'. At the end of the journey they get a security briefing from a two star general who says the violence is decreasing in the country. It is down from 145 attacks a day to 15 attacks a day and these are still mainly due to militia and Al Qaeda. The general says the question of personal safety is up to the individual. Darren thinks the solution for refugees is still resettlement rather than the illegal options. Adam says his own life is easy and now doesn't see them as 'illegal'. Here we see conflicting opinions despite similarity of experience and again we need to examine why this might be so. Subjectivity may come from previous experience as well as current experiences and this colours our perception.

After four weeks the 'experiment is over' and Dr Corlette helps to debrief each of the participants. Darren even admits he has shifted into a more 'compassionate' view of refugees but still doesn't have sympathy for boat people. Gleny thinks 'jumping on a boat' would be her choice. Most agree the problem lies in their original countries but Raquel thinks she can no longer say no to allowing them in. Adam thinks they 'scraped the surface' but it changed him. The refugee issue is 'complex' and their experiences shed some light on the 'humanity' of these people.

No doubt due to their experiences the participants have altered their views to some extent and some offer new ideas on the subject breaking with their previous assumptions and simplistic analysis of the refugee crisis. It is true that they have been manipulated by the director in their experiences but the reality of many of these experiences touches their humanity and the experience of dealing with refugees on a personal level is an altering experience.

Questions for Episode Three

1. What might the 'safety concerns' be in the Kenyan camp? Discuss why their might be some hostility to the participants.

2. What are our first impressions of life in Jordan? Think about this portrayal by the director in the storytelling. Describe the hospital and the condition of the refugees who are being treated.

3. Why is the visit to Deo's home in the permanent camp in Kenya 'bittersweet'?

4. How does this visit show the contrast between those who are lucky and those who are trapped in limbo?

5. Discuss how Raquel's views have changed significantly because of her experiences. Give specific quotes and examples from the text.

6. Why might Rashid be upset during and after his translating duties with his mother? How is emotion used in the series to influence audience and participant opinion?

7. Analyse what each of the participants learn from their trips to Baghdad and the Congo. Why do you think Raquel refuses to participate in the Congo trip?

8. Discuss in detail one assumption you have had challenged from this episode because of the experiences you have seen.

9. Why is there a debrief at the conclusion of the four week experiment?

10. Analyse the full impact of the four week experiment on TWO of the six Australians.

Episode 4 The Response

This episode offers no new footage of the journeys and experiences each of the participants undertook and, in my opinion, no new insights into each of them that we hadn't gleaned from the first three episodes. It begins trying to create a sense of drama by recapping and having a commentator, Anton Enis, talk about how dangerous and controversial the whole thing has been. He calls the show a 'phenomenon' and then says the six Australians are 'brave' before introducing each in turn. The audience is mainly made up of friends and family of the participants plus those that took part and a few invited people who commented on-line.

Gleny makes a significant point when she initially comments,

'I was surprised by some of the elements that were left out'

Darren also expresses concern about the way he was portrayed. Here we need to consider the possible bias of the producers and what they are trying to represent. How realistic is it to edit people's responses to very emotional issues over four weeks in three hours and then expect it to be accurate? It is important to remember that the producers are making television - thus creating a bias which may be a result of the creators' attitudes and values.

We get a long series of clips of Darren who says he was more affected than it showed by what happened to them. Adam says the raid was very upsetting and thinks it would have been worse had the cameras not been there. Darren's wife says the show did not portray him fairly and he is 'kind' which is supported by his work with the Burmese Chin community after his return. Darren is questioned by an African refugee yet he still argues he would not get in a boat. Wasmi, the Iraqi refugee, says he was forced onto a boat because it is so violent at home.

Darren doesn't think anywhere is 'relatively safe' for a refugee. They comment that his journey changed his views and now he is far more sympathetic to their cause. He thinks Jordan is 'shithouse' as a first refuge. They have his parents who were worried about him as they lost all contact. Adam says Villawood Detention Centre was the catalyst that 'shook me up'. They gloss over the violence of the riots there by making it personal with Adam's brother who attended the riots to extinguish the fires. Our moderator then says the controversy created by the show was 'inescapable' and most of it surrounded Raquel.

Raquel 'bore the brunt' of the criticism after the first two episodes but it turned around during the third. Raquel says she 'learnt a lot' from her experience but again we are left to wonder what experiences she had that were omitted because they weren't controversial. She is now more 'open minded' and she admits some of the comments made her 'upset'. Levi, her partner, says that she has told him stories that they omitted and that she is 'kind hearted'. They then show clips from her change of attitude in the final episode. They show comments from people online that show sympathy for Raquel who stopped looking at the comments anyway. Levi says Raquel didn't want to travel before the show and now she is more open and 'grown-up'. The sequence concludes with an invitation from a Muslim woman to visit and become friends. Raquel is the main participant whose change is dramatic and this is in part a response to her extreme and racist views in the initial episodes of the program.

Gleny then says the hurtful comments directed at Raquel needed to be modified by tolerance. She knew Raquel was changed because they had talked in Dubai. Gleny's journey was exciting for her and the show proves we need to be 'more open'. We then shift our attention to Raye who also made a big shift in attitude. She began with controversial comments about 'shooting' refugees and wasn't upset by the drownings at Christmas Island, 'serves the bastards right'. She makes a dramatic change through the course of the month and has befriended the Masudi family. She has been deeply moved by the experience and she feels it is wrong coming home and leaving people behind with 'nothing'.

Raye's husband Peter said she needed to go on the journey because she was involved with the situation because of the detention centre across from her home. We learn that from the camp only 900 out of 84000 people were resettled and Raye thinks this is poor. Roderick says he developed a deeper understanding of the issue and tells how some of the stories he heard were horrific. He found it hard to process a lot of the information from the experiences he had. He gets a question about his T-shirts and his Liberal Party affiliations which he responds to and gets a rousing round of applause.

We also finally get a rundown of what happened to some of the people they met and which people touched them the most. We learn Maisara's sister has won a visa to America while Deo waits in the Kenyan camp for his visa. The Iraqi men have had no success and the families of the men are waiting while the mother has some hope after the programme. Dr Corlett says the programme was valuable because it opened debate. We need to look at the representation and how the content was directed to influencing audience opinion.

Questions for Episode 4 - The Response

1.   What is the purpose of this fourth episode?

2.   Why is the introduction designed to be dramatic and increase the tension? What sort of experience does this opening suggest to an audience? Discuss why the director might wish to represent his ideas in this way.

3.   Why does Darren feel his portrayal was not accurate? Do you agree with him? Think about how he was represented and positioned during the series and why he may have been portrayed that way. Why might the appearance of 'different' characteristics and ideas (values) in the participants helped the narrative of the show?

4.   How does Adam now feel about the refugee problem after his experience? What did he discover through all

the experiences he has undertaken? Does he change his opinions significantly?

5. Raquel's change was the most profound. Discuss this change and what effect it has had on her life. Consider now he she is more open to new experiences and ideas.

6. Do you think the producers may have edited Raquel's story to make it more dramatic and profound? Think about what her boyfriend, Levi says about her story and his experiences of her change. Does his opinion change your perception of her?

7. Gleny changes the least. Does she make any alterations to her ideas and pre-conceptions due to her experiences in the documentary?

8. Raye also has a profound change. Why did she choose to take on the experience initially according to her husband? What experience allows her to discover how she really feels? Are there more than one? Discuss in detail using specific references to the text

9. What specific discovery does Rod comment on? Why is he of particular interest to the audience and the director? Discuss the objectivity of his portrayal and the politicisation of his character.

10. Was this episode useful to the understanding of the issue or do you think the producers were just exploiting the controversy? Did you experience anything new from this episode that might change the way you saw the issue, the participants or the representation of the narrative?

SETTING

Christmas Island

Christmas Island is a territory of Australia and houses an 800 bed detention centre to assist in stopping the 'boat people' from continuing their journey to Australia. Landing there does not  allow automatic entry into Australia and people have been moved from here to other nations such as Papua New Guinea. Prior to the Howard Government's actions the island was a staging post for refugees from Indonesia. Nearly 8000 asylum seekers have been processed on Christmas Island over the last four years.

Iraq

Iraq is a Middle Eastern country. Baghdad is the capital. There has been conflict in Iraq since 2003 when the Allies invaded to remove Saddam Hussein. More recently the war in Syria has spilled over  into the country. Millions of Iraqis have fled the conflict to safe havens such as Jordan.

The Democratic Republic of Congo

The Dark Continent

This term is a nineteenth century nomenclature used to describe Africa. This title came from the habit mapmakers had of leaving the unexplored, interior regions of Africa dark or black. Stanley, the explorer, used this term in the title of his book which gave it wider exposure. Some still use the term today.

Colonisation and Africa

- African nations have been colonised from ancient times as far back as the Greeks and also men like Alexander the Great. The Romans also made inroads under Julius Caesar and Augustus, who established a colony and a capital.

- Vandals were a large East Germanic tribe or group of tribes that first appear in history inhabiting present-day southern Poland. In the 5th century Vandals successively established kingdoms in the Iberian Peninsula and then North Africa. *(WIKI)*

- In the early period of modern European colonisation the focus was mainly on uninhabited regions and island locations. They established forts and kept to the coastline, leaving the interior unexplored.

- This began to change when the established European empires began to grab large tracts of land for themselves and by 1885 the Berlin Conference formally established imperial boundaries in Africa. The countries of France, Britain, Portugal, Germany, Belgium, Spain and Italy all claiming portions for themselves.

- Each country had a different method of rule and while slavery became less common as time passed there was still a formidable trade. Most countries were in Africa for the financial gain, as were the men, but other reasons for colonisation used were exploration, the spreading of Christianity and 'civilising' the savages given as reason for this unprecedented land grab.

- As time moved on the countries of Africa acquired independence and this happened more rapidly after the Second World War. In some countries there was a long war over control with the European power.

- Even today some areas of Africa remain under European control but this is generally limited to islands off the mainland.

King Leopold II and the Belgian Congo

The Congo was first explored by Europeans in 1482. The Congo River was a magnet for trade but it wasn't until 1877 and Henry Morton Stanley's three year expedition the scope of the river was known. As part of the European land grab King Leopold II of Belgium asked Stanley to found a colony in the Congo and begin trade.

The 1855 Berlin Conference ratified this colony and the Congo Free State was born.

While Leopold never went to the Congo his rule has gone down in history as the most appalling and atrocious of all European colonisers. He was an abject failure as a man and administrator as he was only motivated by avarice. It was under his rule that atrocities such as the cutting off of hands and heads were accepted and committed. It has been estimated that ten million native Africans died under his rule but estimates go as high as thirty million in a period from 1885 to 1908.

The Congo was the only African colony under one man's rule. He treated it as a private fiefdom and his only aim was to get as much as he could out of the country. The forced labour used for rubber, mining and the ivory trade were the main cause of deaths.

Under his command traders were allowed to use slave labour, take hostages, chain, starve, and rape the indigenous population. They burned villages and whipped the people with a chicotte (hippo hide whip) as general measures to enforce compliance. This destroyed the strong African kingdom that already existed along the Congo. Conrad's fictional character in *Heart of Darkness*, Kurtz, according to Baffour Ankomah in *New African* (October 1999) is based on Leon Rom a Belgian trader,

> 'Rom's brutality knew no bounds. It was such that even the white people working with him were shocked to the boots...he had...the reputation of having killed masses of people for petty reasons...a flower bed ringed with human heads...a gallows permanently erected in front of the station'.

The brutality of the Belgian regime was so great that there was an international outcry against it and eventually Leopold was forced to sell the country to the Belgian government. This did not improve things for the Africans as the government wanted its money back by gouging all it could from the country.

Leopold's reign is only remembered for his crimes against the African peoples and self – aggrandizement. He enacted laws which required local tribes people to work for forty hours a week free for him, food requisitioning and military service. His use of 'discretionary powers' where he delegated to thugs who could exceed quotas led to 'unrivalled barbarism'. Leopold tried to hide his atrocities by burning the archives of the Congo Free State.

The Congo was finally made independent in 1960 but as only thirty African graduates was trained and in the country there was little preparation for the handover. As well as this there were only 5 African administrators in the country out of five thousand positions. The Belgian government left no infrastructure or skilled people and so the country fell into civil war and chaos. The country changed its name to Zaire but back again. Leopold's legacy is one of the true horror stories of Africa. The Congo is still an incredibly unstable nation and has over one and a half million displaced people constantly moving from the wars and other atrocities committed in that country.

Kakuma Refugee Camp

Kakuma, we are told in the narration is Swahili for "nowhere". Looking at the footage it is an apt description of the huge camp where hopelessness seems rife despite the apparent safety. The Camp in far north-west Kenya has a population of over 90,000 people fleeing the escalating violence in Africa.

Jordan

Between 700,000 and a million refugees from Iraq live in Jordan, a generally prosperous Arab state. Jordan is home to millions of refugees from Syria, Palestine and other Arab states. Over a million of these are illegal workers and the rest have little chance of anything more than safety.

Malaysia

Malaysia is home to one of the largest urban refugee populations in the world. The country has refugees from the Indonesia, Philippines, Vietnam, Cambodia,  Laos, Burma and other Asian countries like Bangladesh, Pakistan, Nepal, Sri Lanka, India and China. The main problems surround Muslims from other countries who gain legal status illegally and in the past Vietnamese boat people who flooded the country after the Vietnam War. If caught refugees are imprisoned, caned and deported. Recently there has been a period of amnesty to try and correct some problems.

Australia

The map on the following page gives Australia its context in the Asia-Pacific region and gives you an idea of the distances and danger involved in these boat journeys. Australia does have an obligation to take refuges under international agreements and as we see from the series the problem of illegal immigrants / asylum seekers is a complex one and has no simple responses.

Source: CartoGIS Services, College of Asia and the Pacific, The Australian National University

Questions for the Setting

- Choose ONE of the countries that form a setting for *Go Back To Where You Came From* and research the refugee problem there. Try to discover the underlying causes of refugees fleeing to that country and that countries response to the problem.

  You can also consider the world / United Nations response to the problem. Have you discovered any solutions to the issue from your viewing of the series? Did the experience of watching these episodes alter the way you see the issue of boat people?

CHARACTER ANALYSIS

- Gleny Rae
- Raye Colbey
- Raquel Moore
- Darren Hassan
- Adam Hartup
- Roderick Schneider

Gleny Rae, singer from Newcastle NSW

> 'I think we have the capacity to take more refugees.'

Gleny is the participant who makes the least changes and makes the least change because of her experiences as she begins at a point of sympathy with the plight of the refugees. She is portrayed as the voice of reason and common-sense by the director and because of this is probably the least interesting participant as there is no conflict or self-growth surrounding her. We see throughout her empathic and sympathetic reaction to both the refugees / asylum seekers and to the other participants. One example of this is the way she responds to Raquel at Kuala Lumpur airport. When Gleny suggests Raquel wear something more appropriate Raquel rebukes her and she accepts it graciously. Another example is from the beginning of the series we see her saying that she would love to have a refugee stay in her own home. She is very sympathetic to the refugees and is shocked by their conditions. She says of the Burmese Chin,

> 'it's almost like a detention centre they've created themselves for their own safety.'

When all the conflict occurs on the 'leaky boat' journey she is nearly invisible on camera which reinforces her portrayal as a sensitive person, which she may well be. Gleny is more than the cipher that she is portrayed by the creators. She is a vibrant personality, a musician and a teacher. Her domestic lifestyle involves semi-rural activities like keeping chickens in her Queensland home. She is quite aware of the way the director and the editors of the series have tried to influence the impact of the series on the audience. She comments in the final studio episode about how much the director, editors etc. have left out. She also has skills as we see when she teaches the children at the school in Kuala Lumpur and her joy at doing this.

Gleny is there in the series but as she already has empathy with the plight of the refugees. Her views don't change much so this doesn't make great television. The other characters have complete turnabouts in their views so their contribution is more dramatic. She doesn't make outrageous statements like some of the others. Gleny is the voice of reason and reason doesn't make tense, conflicting television. Gleny learns and evolves as each little experience she has with the refugees and their world deepens her beliefs. She says she was 'deeply affected' by her experience and this is clear when we see her responses.

Raye Colbey, retired social worker from Inverbrackie South Australia

> 'When the boat crashed coming into Christmas Island I thought, 'it served you bastards right'.'

Raye makes a real change in her opinions which have been coloured by the wonderful treatment that the boat people receive in the detention centre across the road from her home in the Adelaide hills. She says of them in the beginning,

> 'I could go over there right now with a gun and shoot the lot of them. I don't care how hard it is where they come from, I don't think they have the right to come here and demand - *demand* - all this freedom.>

Raye is so involved with the issue her husband tells us in the final episode that she was damaging her health and needed a new perspective. Her initial reaction to the refugee issue is strong and very outspoken. Raye is quite articulate and coherent in her thoughts but she has a great change in her views after staying with in Albury with the Masudi's. She relates to Maisara's story and identifies with her miscarried baby story. From this moment Raye's opinions begin to mellow significantly and we learn in the final episode that she is having the son stay with them. Raye says,

> 'They are real refugees. They came the right way.'

Raye also develops attachments to the Chin Burmese children, especially a couple of girls. We also see her deep attachment to Bahati's brother, Deo, his wife Yanni and Maisara's sister, Amenata in Kakuma. Here she becomes quite emotional as they leave wondering why they are stuck in such a place and cannot find a place to live. Certainly Raye experiences a newfound empathy with the plight of the refugee and has also discovered something about herself through these experiences - a certain peace of mind and she certainly is more calm and relaxed in Episode Four.

Raquel Moore, unemployed from western Sydney

'If it was up to me, I'd send them back. They wouldn't be staying here.'

Raquel creates the best television with her outspoken opinions and her views. One example might be,

'I don't like Africans. You go to Blacktown...and now it really is Blacktown.'

Raquel has very firm views against refugees, especially boat-people and has trouble adjusting to life as one. She notices the 'unhygienic odour' of the places she visits and keeps stating that she is 'Australian' and thus not from there. Raquel makes for great television and they allow her to state her provocative views which demonise her for many left leaning viewers. We learn in the last episode that she caused the most controversy in the tweets and comments the show generated, yet it is Raquel that makes the most of her experiences out of all of the participants.

It is her transformation from an anti refugee protagonist to refugee sympathiser that was the best received part of the episodes. From racist to an individual who says she has a 'heart' and recognises she is 'really badly spoilt' Raquel transforms from her experience totally and fully. She achieves the outcome that the director wanted from the show; Raquel is the change that many would want in the community. Raquel discovers much on her journey and this is especially so in relation to herself. These discoveries come through travel and expanding out of her comfort zone. Her stay with the African family in Albury begins her transformation and we see her eat the food despite her reservations. Here she also discovers their humanity and some of hers.

In Kuala Lumpur she is again confronted by a vastly different culture to the western suburbs of Sydney and finds the conditions unhygienic. Despite this she begins to find connections with people, although on the raid we see her still opinionated in her statements in illegals. One can see her logic but in the face of the human aspect it is hard to maintain this and she eventually begins to change fully in Kakuma where conditions are even worse and people are condemned to lives in limbo. It is here she finds her heart,and on camera proclaims her beliefs and attitudes had completely changed.

In the final episode she is questioned fully and is praised for her changed attitudes. A Muslim woman invites her to befriend her and learn about her religion. Generally she is heartily praised for her turnaround and the public comments have changed from abuse to considerable approbation. Raquel's experiences outside her comfort zone lead to changes in her own behaviours and attitudes. She experiences empathy and tolerance and her own place in the world. Her participation opens up a whole new world of experiences for her and her partner, Levi.

Darren Hassan, businessman from Adelaide

> 'People who come here without any documentation by boat should be immediately expatriated.'

Darren comes into the series with some strong views on refugees yet can never be accused of being racist. He sees things in black and white. Being an ex-soldier, Darren has a clear idea of how he views Australia and its sovereign rights. He cannot entertain the idea that people would leave their families and risk their lives to escape from a safe haven,

> 'Once they leave Malaysia, and then Indonesia, they become economic migrants. We need to send a tougher signal. People who are destroying documents, what are they trying to hide?'

Darren doesn't change this view and has strong reasons, for him, to maintain the view. It is also Darren who comments that the participants are being emotionally manipulated into 'forced empathy' with the migrants. He still considers them economic refugees when they leave a safe haven. He basically has to prove he has sympathy for the plight of the refugees and in a rooftop interview in Jordan he emphasises to the audience,

> 'I am emotionally affected.'

Darren sticks to his ideas and philosophy throughout the episodes and only apologises once for his actions during the raid in Malaysia, blaming his army training for kicking in. In the final episode we learn, from his wife, how since returning he has made contact with the Burmese Chin community and offered assistance. This is a more positive and practical effort than all of the others combined. Darren recognises that the debate has many grey areas and doesn't shift from what he considers to be a sound position. He can't at any point see that these 'boat people' need to take the risk when they are safe.

So this leaves the question, what does Darren experience? He discovers the human, personal side of the refugee equation and this develops his ideas. He has experienced situations that develop his empathy with their situation, especially the Chin's, who he is materially assisting. Darren also understands and enunciates that his experience is being manipulated and alerts viewers to this. We need to consider how this might affect the representation of the issue and the individual.

Adam Hartup, Cronulla lifeguard

> 'Instead of harbouring them, we should just put them straight on a plane and send them back.'

Adam changes his position significantly over the course of the episodes and while he begins with statements such as;

> 'Why didn't the boat people stay in Malaysia or Indonesia where they were in no danger?'

He develops an empathy and sympathy with the plight of the refugee, later saying things such as, 'these guys have nothing' and

> 'I just hope every one of these guys get resettled very, very shortly.'

Adam becomes very involved with the plight of each of the groups he stays with and also sees the simmering violence in the Villawood Detention Centre. His visit there was a 'wake-up call' but his biggest responses are to the Chin and the hospital visit in Jordan. Adam experiences the reality of the fact that these refugees are in 'no-man's-land' and have little hope and nothing economically. He is shocked the Chin work for food and shelter only and can't even contemplate what would happen if the Chin were the victims of the raid in Malaysia, an experience that changes his attitude significantly showing us that perhaps one meaningful experience can change a lifetime of attitudes and less persuasive and emotive experiences.

Adam changes his views from being anti-boat person to an individual who states he would;

> 'Do the journey. Get on the boat. I...I wouldn't live in this.
> If I had to spend 3, 6, 12 months in a detention centre...
> well, if there's a glimmer of hope that I'd be getting out of
> this hole, well of course I would.'

Adam's series of experiences away from Cronulla shows significant change and adaptation to new information gleaned from these experiences.

The quintessential 'Aussie bloke' who has been quite sheltered in the 'Shire' is opened up to a new vision of the world and what the situation is for these people. He discovers much about himself as he evolves his views and thinks about equity. Adam is a likeable, knockabout bloke and his views after his experience on the show surprise his family.

Roderick Schneider, financial planner from Brisbane

'I'm a government-hating, freedom-loving, centre-right winger.'

Roderick 'Rod' Schneider is a member of the Liberal Party and running for office in that organisation. He is an individual with strong views and doesn't want to come across as a 'leftie'. His wardrobe which consists mainly of T-shirts with right wing slogans and graphics support this view. He states categorically he didn't choose them specifically for the show it's just his wardrobe.

With his political affiliations one might have expected him to be completely anti-refugee. He is not rabidly right wing or alt-right but has firm beliefs about the world. His political views and life experiences shape his ideas about an acceptable world order. Despite this he has empathy with the plight of the people he encounters and states,

'We're all refugees.'

and when they go on the raid in Malaysia to the building site he says;

'I hope they're bad, bad people.'

because if they aren't it would be cruel to arrest them. Roderick is a pragmatist and he is clear about his own self-image. He admits that he is 'soft' in the Western world sense as he is a 'desk jockey' and the worst thing that could happen to him at work is a 'paper cut'.

Note how he continues to work in this episode despite the blisters. The other factor that we need to consider when discussing Roderick is that he has never travelled before so any new place is a unique experience for him.

Considering some of the places they are taken to Roderick adapts well and takes a considered position based on these new experiences. For example in Kakuma when Raye is saying the people need more food he points out that it would be nice in a perfect world but who is going to pay for it and recognises;

'You're not going to be pleased but that's the situation.'

Roderick discovers much over the course of the four episodes and comes across as a thoughtful and balanced person who uses his experience in the documentary to adapt his views and his perspective on the world without sacrificing his core beliefs.

Character Questions

- For each character create a table that answers the following questions about discoveries in the text. This will clarify your ideas. In the next column give an example and in the next a specific quote(s). Help for these answers are also included in the themes section which follows.

Question	Example	Quote
What does the character discover about themselves?		
What does the character discover on their travels?		
What does the character discover about ONE specific group of refugees / asylum seekers		
State TWO changes that occur in this character due to one or more discoveries through the series.		

THEMES

- Human Experiences in *Go Back to Where You Came From*
- Discovery in Human Experiences
- Human Experiences and the Journey
- Human Experiences and the Concept of Freedom

Human Experiences in *Go Back to Where You Came From*

'I am emotionally affected.'

We see a number of challenging experiences in the documentary series *Go Back to Where You Came From* and each experience compounds into a larger experience. We have already established much about the content and context of the series in terms of this Common Module but a quick recap here is vital to enable you to focus on the rubric in your response. There can be no doubt that the series was designed to provoke new ideas and challenge assumptions by challenging six disparate individuals to experience the life of and lives of refugees.

If we examine the rubric we can see the collective experiences can be ascribed to both the refugees and the six participants but we can also glean individual experiences and reactions to these experiences. The human qualities that are exhibited such as resilience and understanding provoke strong emotions, especially when we see the physical suffering in war zones, the dearth of hope for children and the anonymity of being in limbo for years. These draw strong emotions and incite reflection as the representations are designed to encourage empathy. The director represents strong positions at the start and the documentary is designed to alter these kind of perceptions.

We hear early on comments such as,

> 'I could go over there right now with a gun and shoot the lot of them. I don't care how hard it is where they come from, I don't think they have the right to come here and demand - *demand* - all this freedom.'

But these alter as the experiences mount up and push the participants into positions of empathy and sympathy. What is interesting is how O'Mahoney gives us the experiences of the refugees and allows them to relate their stories and motivations for fleeing their own country. This allows us to understand the inconsistency of endangering your family to flee a country and travel by boat to Australia. The anomaly of this is explained and we can begin to comprehend the emotional and physical pressure these people are under making the intellectual decision to just move into the uncertain.

Many of the experiences we see on *Go Back to Where You Came From* are negative ones such as the raid, the camps and the personal tales of treatment in the home countries of the refugees. What can we glean from this as human experiences? The individuals seem to have an amazing resilience and their ability to survive in extremely difficult circumstances says much about the attitudes and human qualities that can be found in people after these experiences. We see people who are prepared to do anything to survive and this explains the motivation they have for getting on a boat and risking death to escape from their circumstances. You can track any number of experiences that make individuals leave their home country and then their experiences that shape them and their attitudes to the world. Now we will take a closer look at ways in which these human experiences shape both the people and the documentary.

Discovery in Human Experiences

> 'The big problem for this world is...to educate the system to touch – to touch heart. If I touch your heart, immediately you are able to understand me.'

Deo Masudi – Kakuma refugee

There are many experiences we see throughout the four episodes of *Go Back to Where You Came From* and we will begin our analysis with what the six participants learn about themselves. The quote above from Deo Masudi is central to this as each of the participants has their heart touched in some way. Each learns something about themselves, even if it is just an empathy with people that they didn't understand. The situations they find themselves in are life-changing and thy discover much about themselves including how resilient they are. One example is when Darren admits he is touched by what he has seen and Raquel finds that she is 'spoilt'.

While some of the six don't discover as much about themselves as others each one grows and changes in some way and evolves and develops their views and perceptions of the issue. Raquel turns around from being racist and disliking black people to having a clear understanding of the hardships of the Masudi's and also the Chin. Each participant has to deal with things way beyond their comfort zone from physical hardship, lack of sleep to strange foods and long distance travel. The discoveries they make from these experiences are evident in the fourth episode when they debrief in front of an audience.

Here it is interesting to hear how their families saw the change in each participant. Darren's wife tells of his empathy and how he rarely shows emotion – something that was an issue during filming. Raye's husband tells of her changed health and mental condition once she discovered the real issues rather than rant at the detention centre across the road. Levi, Raquel's partner, tells of her big heart which finally changed her views and that her experiences travelling made her discover a love of travel. Adam's parents also talk of how his experiences changed him and widened his views on the world.

Each of the participants discovered something about refugees they didn't know prior to their experience. While Gleny was sympathetic she learnt the terrible conditions which they live and this reinforced her ideas. This raises the issue of the experiences around place by each of the individuals participating in the experiment. The geographical distances they encountered on their journey certainly affected them. Look at the leaky boat sequence in the first episode when they are faced with the eternity of the sea and an unknown destination. It is interesting for the audience that the participants are not allowed learn where they are going until specific moments in the episode to increase tension. This is the impact and power of an experience into the unknown.

Another unknown is what they will face when they arrive. The initial destinations are still in Australia and only the circumstances are uncomfortable. Things are outside their comfort zones but not too far and it does give them an opportunity to adapt to different conditions. We see some struggle to adapt, for example, Raquel with her 'hygiene' issues and the shocked expression of all three women when they are told that 'fifty' women live in the room when they stay with the Burmese Chin in Kuala Lumpur. As the series progresses the geographical stresses on the six become more extreme and they learn to experience their inner strength although Raquel doesn't venture to the Congo, discovering her limitations.

When we discuss the geographical/location issues that the participants undergo it certainly is worth analysing the issues facing the refugees similarly. They have been displaced geographically and, unlike the participants, don't know they will be going home. They too discover new places and cultures and have little or no economic assistance until they arrive in a country such as Australia. Their resilience is also sorely tested but many have just now experienced the happiness of a safe place. Think about the stresses on them, many with families, in unfamiliar environments. Also consider the fact they are stateless and have little hope of resettlement. Even if they are safe from war, rape and starvation they have little future and this leads to hopelessness.

At this point we can also contemplate the discoveries of the audience. The narration by Friels gives us some information which may be startling to some. It gives us context and historical detail as well as statistical information which informs and builds a picture of the whole around the individual examples we see on screen. It allows us to develop opinions based on factual information while the emotive strings are being tugged on by the individuals involved. This is not to say the narration isn't emotive and for evidence of this read techniques section. Think about what you discovered from viewing each of the episodes and how this affected your perspective, if at all.

Now I would like to explore some other ideas that you can link to human experience with *Go Back to Where You Came From.*

Human Experience and the Journey

Journeys are another way of participating in and describing experiences. The journeys can be physical such as the plane flights or the boat trip at sea but they can also be personal intellectual and emotional journeys. Some like Raye have significant moments on their journey such as her learning that Maisara had lost a daughter due to her inability to afford medicine in the camps. Others like Raquel take more time and her views evolve on the journey. Others such as Darren take him to absorb the experiences they have and then evaluate them based on their own philosophy of life.

Remember too that the whole basis of the series is about journeys – the journeys of the asylum seekers as they try to establish a new life. The documentary makers also take each of the participants and us on a journey to experience the life of an asylum seeker / refugee, an experience none of us would have encountered in our lives. The journey is a great way to show different and unique experiences and it is effective here as we get deeper into the various experiences that the participants face in each episode.

Human Experiences and Freedom

Another aspect of human experiences that you can use for *Go Back to Where You Came From* is the search for freedom and it can also be linked to the concept of the storytelling in the documentary tradition to give some unity to your essay in the this module. Each of the participants gets freedom to form their views and the freedom to express those views. They have experiences that change how they see freedom and what freedom really is – perhaps the experience of losing freedom makes them see how valuable that it is.

They and we, experience the Chin in a prison of their own making in the slums of Kuala Lumpur because they hunger for freedom eventually. Each of the experiences the six have revolved around discovering why these people search for freedom so avidly and accept so many dangers to succeed. Perhaps we might conclude that the concept of freedom is hope for these people and they are willing to risk their lives and those of their families for it.

LANGUAGE

Documentary Techniques

The techniques used in a documentary are designed to create emotional pertinence and control over an audience. To do this the director and his team have to 'show not tell' with pictures and allow the audience to find their way. To assist this process a narration is often used. The narration must be relevant, simple and linked to the visuals and is usually, as in studying this text, either first person narration as opposed to the third person omniscient narrator or the 'voice of God'. In *Go Back to Where You Came From* we have a hosted narration in parts, a third person for the footage and in parts the narrator is on screen when 'refugee expert' Corlett is presenting. The narration from actor Colin Friels is often emotive for what is presumed to be a detached omniscient narrator. For example in the second episode he says things such as, 'living in squalor', 'shadow world of refugees', 'limbo existence' and the 'guide' Corlett repeats the 'squalid' concept just in case you missed it as he narrates.

Also when you watch each episode think about the 'set-up' that they include the audience in and the 'pay off' at the conclusion. This is where the tension is created through the idea and counter-idea. In *Go Back to Where You Came From* the idea is based around the comments from one or more of the participants about refugees/boat people and then the episode sets out to disprove or change that view. In the case of refugees the director must also be sensitive to their needs and values as they have been, at times, placed under tremendous strain. Thus the camera work cannot be obtrusive and invasive. Think about the interview with Maisara when she tells of the suffering of her family and how both her sisters were raped. The camera moves in close to capture her expressions but also cuts away.

This raises the question of what to show which a director has control of and indeed the duration of shots, scenes and the episode itself. Obviously conflict is better television and one example of this is in Episode One when the conflict between Raye and Raquel on the fake refugee boat makes compelling television but has little to do with the issue of refugees. Yet their swearing, arguing and threats of violence makes the show effective. Also examine the introductory piece to each episode about 'the issue that divides a nation', 'strong views' and 'dangerous' that add to the drama. Even Raquel's statement 'I am a bit racist' is inflammatory. With these decisions about what to show comes a responsibility and this again raises the issue of bias in the four episodes we have to consider.

The issue of bias has been mentioned before and certainly *Go Back to Where You Came From* has been accused of bias in its presentation and representation of the issue. Yet it is up to the audience how much this bias affects them and their viewing experience.

In a thoughtful article *You call this even-handed? Refugee series is strictly for the gullible*, in the *Sydney Morning Herald* Paul Sheehan writes,

> 'While the quality of the filmmaking is good, the laudatory descriptions of the program as being even-handed are over-stated. It is stacked with commentary, from the narration, to the structure, to the guide, Dr David Corlett, who is immersed in the refugee industry...'

Sheehan also points to the perceptive questions asked by the participants that are never answered. In response to this criticism O'Mahoney has stated in an article in *The Australian* newspaper with Graeme Blundell that his position was a neutral one,

> 'Even those of the six who didn't change positions came to appreciate the discussion is not as simple as they had always thought...I don't want viewers to think that we want to manipulate them into being extremely welcoming of any asylum-seekers or we have a position that they are all bad and unwelcome.'

He goes on to state that he feels *Go Back to Where You Came From* is 'a kind of blend between reality TV and observational documentary.'

The final decision must lie with the audience and it is intriguing to read some of the blogs and tweets at the time of airing which are quite extreme from both the left and right. For us the main concern is how these techniques show human experiences and support the ideas in the text. Look for specific examples of how when the participants experience something about life as an asylum-seeker they are shown in close-up with expressive, often teary faces as they experience the issue. Examples of this might be when Adam visits the hospital with the bomb victims in Jordan. Another is Raye departing from the camp in Kenya. This series uses emotive shots to show how affected the participants are by their experience and the experiences are designed to do this. Darren even notes in the show how they are being manipulated to show empathy.

The director also uses long shots, long-wide shots to orientate the audience to particular unfamiliar locations. This is more so in the foreign locations but he also does some of this with the Liverpool and Albury locations. It is clever direction to give orientation particularly to places many Australians would not have experienced such as Kakuma, Goma and Bahgdad. We need also to note how the music over the visuals impacts on how we perceive that situation. One particularly good example of this is when the raid occurs in Malaysia. Listen to how dramatic the music is and when it cuts in and out to add to the scene. In the third episode note how the music is ominous as they discuss Kakuma and the shots of isolation and poverty. Just as they queue for food the sounds of the camp are overlaid by the narration, 'they are escaping death, torture, rape and starvation...there are many hungry mouths but little food...'. Think about how this positions the audience. Note also, as in episode two, when they are heading into a Malaysian city how the music is Arabic in sound to highlight the Muslim nature of the country which has already been seen in the dress, 'every woman is wearing a tea towel'.

Go Back to Where You Came From – The Response is slightly different from the other episodes in that it is filmed entirely in a studio with a set and audience. We do get a recount of the experience to orientate viewers but there is no new footage, just a rehashing of bits of episodes. There is less conflict in this episode as the characters have basically come around to the point of view of the director, even the once 'racist' Raquel who has come to rethink her position. Even the harder questioning of Darren who still has many valid points doesn't have the same impact. Compare how he is treated to Raye who comments 'I was surprised by some of the elements that were left out' but was already supportive of refugees. Also note the questioning of Roderick about his T-shirts because they don't hold the same leftist views as the production staff.

The role of Anton Enus in this episode is intriguing as he recaps and tries to make the debate interesting, describing the show as a 'phenomenon'. Watch how they cut to him nodding and looking wise in close up as he responds to answers. Still a debate has been started and if we consider the purpose of a documentary to inspire change and challenge and audiences beliefs then the experience has been successful. Do you think that the series has created debate and inspired change? What did you experience from your viewing? Was it a major experience that for you that led to change, a 'life -changing experiment' or something lesser?

Finally we need to consider the series as a whole and how effective these techniques and ideas are over time. As a documentary it was timely as the issue was and perhaps still is of import in Australia. How long do you think its shelf life or longevity is? How relevant will it be in five years when another group of students will be studying it for the HSC? Will the experiences and attitudes that the participants and audience developed from it be impactful over time?

Questions for Language Elements

- Discuss the impact of the narration and the effect of multiple forms of narration. How does the narrator guide the audience through the experience being undertaken? Think about some of the narration and discuss how subjective it is. How does this subjectivity belie the concept of the objective documentary?

- Analyse how much reality style filming is used in one episode and the manner in which it is edited. What other techniques are used in each episode? We need to remember that some of the participants feel that they were edited selectively and were portrayed incorrectly. Do you think from your experience watching the documentary that this is true / possible / incorrect?

- Analyse the role and use of music in two scenes from different episodes. How does the music help represent ideas?

- How does the use of refugees change from episode to episode? How do you feel that they are represented in the series? Is the portrayal realistic or over-dramatised for television?

- Describe Kakuma and how each of the participants responds to the situation. How do you perceive Kakuma?

- Discuss the Baghdad scenes and how the city is portrayed. Look at all aspects of the filming and the use of American military personnel.

- Comment on the shots used in TWO specific scenes from different episodes and how they contribute to the idea of human experiences.

- Episode Four is very different. How do you see its construction and portrayal of the participants?

- How does the narrative over three episodes help us, as an audience, experience elements of refugee life?

THE ESSAY

The essay consists of the basic form of an introduction, body paragraphs and conclusion. The esssay has been the subject of numerous texts and you should have the basic form well in hand. As teachers, the point we would emphasise would be to link the paragraphs both to each other and back to your argument (which should directly respond to the question). Of course, ensure your argument is logical and sustained.

Make sure you use specific examples and that your quotes are accurate. To ensure that you respond to the question, make sure you plan carefully and are sure what relevant point each paragraph is making. It is solid technique to actually 'tie up' each point by explicitly coming back to the question.

When composing an essay the basic conventions of the form are:

- State your argument, outline the points to be addressed and perhaps have a brief definition.

A solid structure for each paragraph is:
- Topic sentence (*the main idea and its link to the previous paragraph/ argument*)
- Explanation/ discussion of the point including links between texts if applicable.
- Detailed evidence (*Close textual reference – quotes, incidents and technique discussion.*)
- Tie up by restating the point's relevance to argument/ question

- Summary of points
- Final sentence that restates your argument

As well as this basic structure, you will need to focus on:

Audience – for the essay the audience must be considered formal unless specifically stated otherwise. Therefore, your language must reflect the audience. This gives you the opportunity to use the jargon and vocabulary that you have learnt in English. For the audience ensure your introduction is clear and has impact. Avoid slang or colloquial language including contractions (like 'doesn't', 'e.g.', 'etc.').

Purpose – the purpose of the essay is to answer the question given. The examiner evaluates how well you can make an argument and understand the module's issues and its text(s). An essay is solidly structured so its composer can analyse ideas. This is where you earn marks. It does not retell the story or state the obvious.

Communication – Take a few minutes to plan the essay. If you rush into your answer it is almost certain you will not make the most of the brief 40 minutes to show all you know about the question. More likely you will include irrelevant details that do not gain you marks but waste your precious time. Remember an essay is formal so **do not** do the following: story-tell, list and number points, misquote, use slang or colloquial language, be vague, use non-sentences or fail to address the question.

PLAN:

Don't even think about starting without one!

Introduce... the texts you are using in the response *Argument*: The human experience is affected by: • Idea One • Idea Two • Idea Three	You need to let the marker know what texts you are discussing. You can start with a definition but it can come in the first paragraph of the body. You MUST state your argument in response to the question and the points you will cover as part of it. Wait until the end of the response to give it!

$\downarrow$

Idea One – Aspect of human experience as outlined in the textual material, e.g. physical impact. **Idea Two** – Another aspect of human experience as outlined in the textual material, e.g. psychological impact. • explain the idea • where and how is it shown in the prescribed text? • where and how is it shown in related text 1? **Idea Three** – People's sense of experience is affected by context and environment • explain the idea • where and how shown in the prescribed text? • where and how shown in related text 1?	You can use the things you have learned to organise the essay. For each one, you say where you saw this in your prescribed text and where in related text(s). Two or three ideas are usually enough as you can explore them in detail.

$\downarrow$

• Summary of two key ideas • Final sentence that restates your argument	Make sure your conclusion restates your argument. It does not have to be too long.

MODEL ESSAY OUTLINE

> **To what extent are human experiences significant in the set text?**
>
> **From your studies respond to this question using your set text and at ONE piece of other textual material**

This essay needs to be attacked in a manner that responds to the question and shows ALL your knowledge about the text. The question lends itself to a close study of Ivan O'Mahoney's *Go Back to Where You Came From* as the text does show how the human experience is integral to life and how it shapes our other experiences and interaction with the world.

An introduction might be written:

> Human experiences are important in O'Mahoney's *Go Back to Where You Came From* and the two related texts Lawrence's *Jindabyne* and Ed Sheeran's song *Castle on the Hill*. These texts show how human experiences are integral to human existence and bring more meaning to one's life. Life is about experiences that challenge us and define how we see the world. They shape our beliefs and attitudes and can be confronting at the same time. Without experiences our lives would be empty and meaningless.

Your essay should then follow the outlined plan and develop these ideas. This gives you the opportunity to link the texts and fully develop each of the ideas.

ANNOTATED RELATED MATERIAL: DIFFERENT STUDIES OF HUMAN EXPERIENCES

Jindabyne – **Ray Lawrence**

Jindabyne is an Australian film that captures a wide array of human experiences. It touches on the ideas mentioned in the introduction to this text in a number of detailed instances. We can begin by considering the following before beginning a detailed examination of the narrative.

The collective human experience:

- Aboriginality and the spiritual;
- The Fishermen and their code;
- The reaction of the townsfolk;
- Media response;
- Interaction with the natural world.

Individual Experience:

- An individual character's response to the body – choose one;
- The killer;
- Response to the revelations;
- Past experiences and how they impact on current experiences;
- Reaction to loss – emotional;
- Assumptions about life.

We can now look at the plot to help us understand each of these issues. *Jindabyne* begins with the sound of a radio being tuned and the Australian feel of the movie is immediate with the theme music for the ABC news. Lawrence emphasises the isolation by having the radio not tune in correctly for an unknown female character, forcing her to use the cassette player. With this unusual beginning we know that her experience is not going to be positive.

We then pan to the rocks slowly where Gregory, our killer, sits patiently in a truck with the engine running watching the road. We know he is prepared for this as he has binoculars. He sees an Aboriginal girl, Susan O'Connor, driving and she is the one fiddling with the radio. He chases her down and forces her to stop. He moves toward her as we see a long shot of how isolated they are. We see his face in her window looming above her and screaming about the electricity coming down from the mountains. This film is no murder mystery, as we know from the beginning that the murderer is Gregory the electrician. This is about the experiences of the other characters in the film and how they respond to current experiences.

The Kane family, Stewart, Claire and son Tom, is waking. Claire pretends to sleep, before waking suddenly and being affectionate with Tom. Stewart and Tom head out fishing. The scene doesn't feel quite right and there is some emotional tension between Stewart and Claire that is unspoken due to what they have experienced in the past. Claire had a complicated past when she was pregnant with Tom. When she finds she is pregnant again, she becomes emotional and slightly unstable.

As the film builds we see the complex pasts of the characters and their interactions in the confinement of the small town. The fishing trip is a break from this and extremely important in their lives.

We see some of the emotional instability in characters such as Caylin-Calandria, who with Tom, has some issues at school. Along with Caylin-Calandria, Claire and Jude also have issues but in a nicely framed shot of the three female characters, we see them conform as members of a close knit group. The sacrifice they make is similar to Gregory's but on a different scale. Note the connection here and how each one is to get back to order and societal norms. This is the collective experience for all the characters.

At the Kanes' home the tensions are obvious from their past experiences but they contain it for appearances' sake. Occasionally, the tension reaches breaking point and the experience strains the superficial approach. The tension builds at home and the fishing trip seems like a good opportunity to break the cycle.

When we see Gregory dump Susan O'Connor's body in the river, we know that the fishing and her death will interact.

The next morning, the fishermen head off for their one big trip of the year and the sign 'Gone fishing' is put in the garage window. We see Billy on the phone to Elissa and putting the sign the wrong way round in the window shows his immaturity. They have already said they are taking him away to make a man of him. The four men have a few beers on the way and talk as they travel through the landscape. They intend to give Billy the experience they think he needs as a 'man' — a cultural rite of passage.

The men arrive and the high-tension electricity wires punctuate the wilderness. They begin to hike toward the valley. It's a long walk in and the terrain is hilly and difficult. They stop on the way and again we see Billy's naivety when Stewart says 'Listen to that' meaning the silence but he can't, as he has his earphones in. It is part of the break in tension of the film that they commune with nature. This experiential break affects all the men. The episode represents a distinct human experience.

Stewart wanders down the river fishing and sees Susan's body caught in the rocks. Hesitantly, he wades out to it and turns it over saying 'Oh Jesus' repeatedly. He screams for the others to come as he drags the body to the bank. He is obviously upset, making the sign of the cross. Stewart tells Rocco to 'take her, for fuck's sake, take her' and their shock is obvious. They all stare at the body and Billy goes to run off but they stop him. The four men meet and decide to leave her in the water and tie her so she doesn't float away.

The presence of the body threatens to detract from the enjoyment of the fishing experience. The act of attempted isolation of the bad experience is expected to evoke only a mild response. They do not anticipate the stormy reaction it receives when they return to the community.

The men go on fishing, with Stewart getting the first big fish on an absolutely perfect day. The lure of the fish is strong, especially when they see the big one he has caught. They have a successful and enjoyable time, a positive experience. They get a photo of the catch and Billy holds up his fish in a typical hunter/gatherer pose. Capturing an experience this way is most enjoyable.

It is a photo that will come back to haunt them as things change back in the world. An unanticipated adverse reaction can be a horrific experience.

Stewart goes to check on the dead girl, rolling her over and getting debris off her face in a quite tender gesture. The next day they head back and report it. At the car Billy rings Elissa and says they found a body but 'caught the most amazing fish'. They are told by the police to wait and seem despondent their trip has been ruined. They organise their story as Stewart says they have 'to get their story straight'.

We cut to Gregory eating breakfast and he appears to be a normal, lonely man until he goes out to his shed where he has hidden Susan's car and this reminds us of the evil in him. Consider his experience and his motivations. How does he see his actions and the world?

The next day at the station the policeman tells the fishermen 'we don't step over bodies for our recreational pursuits' and 'the whole town's ashamed of you'. When they are told to 'piss off' from the station the press are waiting for them and Billy makes a comment. Carl is angry with the press but we can begin to see signs of distress within the whole group.

The experience they had so looked forward to has become a negative one and the tensions we saw before are exacerbated by the emotional and collective response to the murder. Claire soon becomes obsessed with the whole affair because of her own state. The newspaper the next day has the headline, 'Men fish over dead body' because Billy has talked. Billy is late to work and Stewart tells him they have to 'stick together on this'.

Susan's sister calls them 'animals' and raises the race question by asking if they would have left a white girl. The Aboriginal youths begin to attack and vandalise the property of the men in violent outbursts, including throwing a rock through Billy's van window and thus endangering his baby. They insult Carl at the caravan park and vandalise the garage.

The police aren't any help and the situation deteriorates. Jude tells the police they shouldn't be enforcing the 'political correctness' laws. The intervention of the sense of Aboriginality and race challenges the assumptions people have and how we see the world. The contrasting views are ingrained in the social structures and part of different collective experiences.

The Aboriginal people see the white people as 'interfering' and the group of fishermen begin to fight amongst themselves. Elissa says they shouldn't go to the bush at all as it's sacred. The group talk about the bush and Rocco punches Stewart for saying the Aborigines are superstitious. The experience of racial tension becomes ever-present and adds to the emotional responses to the experience.

We now head slowly to a resolution of the conflict brought about by the various experiences. Each is handled in a different manner by characters and you can explore one or two of the responses. To cycle back to the original murder, Claire is stalked by Gregory in his truck. He stops her but drives off after staring weirdly, an odd experience in itself.

Terry and Stewart talk and Stewart meets Rocco and Carl. He tells them Claire's left him 'again'. Rocco can't believe it and we cross cut to her looking out into the wilderness after he looks thoughtfully out the window. These different reactions to experiences mirror attitudes in life and reactions to emotional and intellectual conflict.

In conclusion, Lawrence takes us back to the healing power of nature in our human experiences when the Aboriginal people are having a ceremony. Gregory watches while Claire walks in. Again we see his truck as an omnipresent force in the film, almost an extension of him. An Aboriginal man tells Claire to 'piss off' from the ceremony after she says she has come to pay her 'respects' but he is told to leave her alone by an Auntie.

The smoke and tribal music symbolise the ceremonial nature of the setting and the camera pans around the scene and the bush. We see parts of the ceremony with chanting and clapping sticks. The camera moves in and out while other shots pan around the bush, giving us the full experience and Lawrence portrays this as a positive, healing experience.

Eventually Stewart, Tom, Carl, Jude and Rocco arrive to pay respects. Tom runs to his mother and Stewart goes over and says 'Sorry' but is rebuffed by the father who throws dirt on him and spits, refusing his apology. Then an Aboriginal girl tells a little about Susan's story and sings the last love song Susan wrote.

The camera pans around all the faces as they listen to the song and the ceremonial smoke wafts around. It seems to have some healing effect on everyone, as it is a meaningful experience which raises the idea of the spiritual experience in the text. The girl stops singing through emotion. 'Be gone' seems to symbolise in language the whole scenario for each character.

We see a long wide shot of the bush before fading back to Gregory waiting again in his car behind the rocks for another victim. It is quite a circular conclusion and it is an odd end when he crushes the fly. We don't quite know what to make of the whole experience and he seems to be the only character unchanged by the experiences in the film.

Poem: 'Inland' by John Kinsella

The poem captures the mood and ethos of the outback farming communities and deals with the human aspect more than some of the other poems in Kinsella's collection: *Peripheral Light*. This poem is one long restless thought that mimics memories and recollection while raising the current, topical issues that concern the poet. As usual with his poems Kinsella orientates the audience early with the word 'Inland' and then continues the poem without a full stop. The poem flows with the use of commas but Kinsella allows us to stop and think with the use of the colon, brackets and the hyphen. Look for these punctuation stops as you read as they emphasise a specific point or idea that resonates with the audience.

The first stanza gives us a foreshadowing of the events to follow with the warnings in the words 'storm', 'alert' and 'uncertain'. This ominous tone is reinforced by the word 'ghosts' and the implication of death which is constant in much of Kinsella's poetry. The next stanza deals with a more human element and we get the country feel with the bracketed gossip about McHenry's accident which shows the close knit community. Habits here are formed as part of survival and known to all as we see 'the old man plying the same track' and the families possibly heading to church on the Sunday morning.

The third stanza returns to the vagaries of nature. Kinsella repeats 'uncertain' with regard to the weather. Weather and the environment play a large role in farming communities and it is especially so at sowing and harvest. Despite the uncertainty and 'ashen' days which alter 'moods', the community returns to their habits and routines which shape their lives. The next stage returns to the road and the implication of a journey but a journey that is straight and in conflict with the cycles of the natural world. The path seems already marked and measured. It is 'straight and narrow', marked by a theodolite.

The final four lines of the poem are pure Kinsella, marking the transience of humanity on the landscape. We read

> 'it's a place of borrowed dreams
> where the marks of the spirit
> have been erased by dust –
> the restless topsoil'

The European farmers had 'borrowed dreams' for their own relationship with the land but this line also harks back to the indigenous Dreamtime when the land was created. The indigenous view that the land owns the people is also true for Kinsella. This sense of nobody owning the land is strong in his poetry. European impact on the land can be seen in the spirituality being removed by the dust—dust created by the poor farming techniques transferred from a different land. He finishes with the 'restless topsoil' as if the whole earth is moving in its own discontented journey, just as the people move.

The influence here of genuinely lost spirituality and connection with the land as we move directly on the 'high road' contrasts with the more flowing, 'restless' side of the natural world. This visual contrast is obvious but we can also discuss the contrast between habit and spirit. 'Inland' is a poem that uses the landscape to show the contrast between two views of the countryside.

DRAMA: Eugene O'Neil's *Desire Under the Elms*

O'Neill sets out to instruct how the house and elms should appear and the year is 1850. Note how he describes the 'enormous' elms as,

> 'exhausted women resting their sagging breasts and
> hands and hair on its roof, and when it rains their tears
> trickle down monotonously and rot on the shingles'

and how they dominate and 'rot'. It is important to read this both in terms of the play and in the context of American theatre. The description here shows O'Neill's genius at new design and original theatricality.

Part One: Scene One

The whole first page and a third are nearly all playwright notes that describe the farm, the house and the characters of Eben, Simeon and Peter. The first words of the play, 'God! Purty!' reflect the beauty of the land and how Eben perceives it. Eben is 'resentful and defensive' and feels 'trapped' on the farm.

His older half-brothers Simeon and Peter are 'more bounce and homelier in face, shrewder and more practical.' They all have worked hard on their father's farm over the years and have little feeling for their absent father. We learn that Simeon had a 'woman who died and that Peter is excited by the prospect of 'gold in the West'. They all talk about how hard they've worked and hope that the father might 'die soon'. What we get from all this is that they are earthy and this is reflected in their bodies and clothes which are all dirt stained.

We also see here the difference between them as Eben sees gold in the pasture, not California, as they head in for a dinner of bacon in what seems a ritual they have performed many times before. Note that O'Neill calls for the use of the curtain at the end of the scene.

Scene Two

It is twilight and again we get detailed notes on the interior scene. Simeon tells Eben he should not wish their father dead and Eben replies he's not his son but, 'I'm Maw – every drop of blood!' He then blames the father, Ephraim Cabot, for killing his mother by working her to death but the others just say there was work to be done. O'Neill gets them to list the jobs and Eben comes back with 'vengeful passion' that, while they did nothing, he will see his mother gets 'rest and sleep in her grave!'

They then discuss Cabot's absence and how he just drove off in a buggy one day in a rush. Simeon says that when he went,

> 'He druv off in the buggy, all spick an' span, with the mare all breshed an' shiny, druv off clackin' his tongue an' wavin' his whip. I remember it quite well'

Eben mocks Simeon for not stopping him and the scene concludes with Eben leaving to see Minnie the town whore. We learn all the Cabot men have slept with her. Simeon and Peter say that Eben is just like 'Paw' and thinks of California. The final image is of Eben with his arms stretched to the sky talking about starts and sin, 'my sin's as purty as any one on 'em!', until he 'strides' to the village for Min.

Scene Three

It is 'pitch darkness' and Eben comes home with the news that Cabot has married a 'purty' thirty-five year old. He has heard this in the village and this effectively disinherits the boys. Simeon and Peter see California as their only option now. Eben tells the boys that they can have three hundred dollars each if they sign their share of the farm over to him. He can get the money as his mother told him,

> 'I know whar it's hid. I been waitin' – Maw told me. She
> knew whar it lay fur years, but she was waitin'....It's her'n
> – the money he hoarded from her farm an' hid from Maw.
> It's my money by rights now.'

They think about it and Eben tells them about his night with Min. He tells how he hates the new wife after the boys suggest he might sleep with her, just like Min, to get the old man back. Peter and Simeon say they'll do the deal and leave the farm. Both are bitter and vindictive about Cabot.

Scene Four

The setting is the same as Scene Two and the boys are discussing how they don't have to work now – it is all down to Eben who is jubilant as he thinks it will all be his. Peter and Simeon again reflect on how like his father he is, 'Like his Paw'. They also tell he isn't much of a milker but they soon talk about their leaving and how they'll miss some aspects of the farm.

Eben comes back in and says that the 'old mule an the bride' are coming. The two older boys begin to pack and sign Eben's papers as he gives them the money Cabot had hidden. They tell him

© Five Senses Education Pty Ltd

they'll send him 'a lump o' gold for Christmas' and head into the yard feeling 'light' because of their newfound freedom.

Ephraim Cabot and Abbie Putnam then come in and O'Neill describes them in detail. Cabot is

> 'seventy-five, tall and gaunt, with great, wiry, concentrated power, but stoop shouldered by toil. His face is hard as if it were hewn from a boulder, yet there is a weakness in it'

but his face is weakened with petty pride. Abbie is

> 'thirty-five, buxom, full of vitality. Her round face is pretty but marred by its rather gross sensuality. There is strength and obstinacy in her jaw, a hard determination in her eyes, and about her whole personality.'

She also has a 'desperate quality'. Cabot shows Abbie the place and she says to him it's 'mine'. Then he sees the two boys not working. He introduces Abbie and she goes to look at 'her' house and they warn her Eben's inside.

Cabot tells them to get to work and they give him cheek, saying they are 'free' and heading to California. They 'whoop' it up and he says he'll have them chained up. They throw rocks at the house, smashing the window and head off singing. Abbie sticks her head out the window and says she likes the room but he is thinking of the stock and 'almost runs' to the barn.

Abbie then meets Eben in the kitchen and talks to him in 'seductive tones'. She says she doesn't want to be his 'Maw' but friends and he cusses her. She tells him of her troubled life and how Cabot gave her a chance to escape it. He calls her a 'harlot' and they argue over ownership of the farm. She has the upper hand in law and he leaves but the seeds of their growing attraction have been set.

Outside he and his father argue about life and work and he tells Eben 'Ye'll never be more'n half a man!' The scene ends with Abbie washing up and the faint notes of the song the boys were singing as they left.

Part Two: Scene One

Again O'Neill describes in detail the farmhouse setting. Two months have passed and it is a hot Sunday afternoon. Abbie in her best outfit is sitting on the porch and Eben comes out of the house also dressed in his best. They stalk each other, both attracted and repelled. As he walks away she 'gives a sneering, taunting chuckle' at him and they argue but the attraction is obvious. She says that nature will pull him to her but he says that she is married and he goes to leave her.

She accuses him of going to Min and she gets angry stating he'll never get the farm,

> 'Ye'll never live t' see the day when even a stinkin' weed on it 'll belong t' ye!'

He says he hates her and leaves as Cabot enters. She tells him Eben has been mocking him and twists the conversation to the inheritance of the farm. She tells him Eben lusts after her and as he angers she backs off in her accusations. Reassured, he says that she can have the farm if she bears the son she says she wants with him. He says that he'd 'do anythin' ye axed, I tell ye!' if she gave him a son and tells her to pray to God for it to happen.

Scene Two

It is about eight in the evening and here the bedrooms are highlighted, with Eben in one and Cabot with Abbie in the other. The two of them are talking about a son. They seem together, yet apart, as he tells her of his life on the farm and how God's hard. He both lost and gained on the way through, but the farm is his. He says he is pleased he found her, his 'Rose o' Sharon'. Abbie promises him that she will bear a son as he basically threatens her,

> 'Ye don't know nothin' – nor never will. If ye don't hev a son t' redeem ye...'

and he leaves to sleep in the barn with the cows 'whar it's restful'.

We then see Eben and Abbie restless and she leaves the room and goes to him. He 'submits' to her kisses then 'hurls' her away. Abbie says she'd make him 'happy' and she knows he wants her too much. She tells him to go down to the parlour and he is shocked as this is where his mother was 'laid out'. She leaves for the parlour and he wonders what's happening. The scene closes with a question to his dead mother, 'Maw! Whar are yew?' but we know that he wants her and will go to her.

Scene Three

The scene now shifts to the parlour which is described as a 'grim, repressed room like a tomb'. Abbie waits and Eben appears and he sits at her invitation. They talk about his Maw and how they hate Cabot. Abbie throws herself at him with 'wild passion' and he is caught up in the moment and thinks that it's his Maw wanting him to sleep with Abbie to get revenge on Cabot,

I see it! I sees why. It's her vengeance on him – so's she kin rest quiet in her grave!

Abbie proclaims her love for him and he for her then they kiss 'in a fierce, bruising kiss' to close the scene.

Scene Four

A more bold and confident Eben leaves the house and Abbie opens the parlour window. She calls him over for a kiss and they talk a bit before Eben says his Maw can now rest. They split as Cabot comes out of the barn but are now obviously in love. Eben tells Cabot that his Maw is now at rest and Cabot says he rests best with the cows. Cabot is confused but the scene ends with him criticising Eben as 'Soft-headed' and a 'born fool' but, being a practical man, he heads for breakfast.

Part Three: Scene One

Time has passed to 'late spring the following year'. Eben is upstairs in emotional and psychological conflict while a party happens downstairs. Cabot has drunk too much and Abbie sits, pale and thin, in a rocking chair. There is a fiddler and Abbie begins the scene by asking for Eben and the guests 'titter' as most think the baby is Eben's, not Cabot's, which is true enough. They laugh and Cabot is angered by this and orders them to dance. The fiddler 'slyly' says they're waiting for Eben but Cabot mocks the boy and then ensues a bawdy conversation about his fertility,

I got a lot in me – a hell of a lot – folks don't know on. Fiddle 'er up, durn ye! Give 'em somethin' t' dance t!'

The fiddler plays and they dance. Cabot joins in frantically and 'whoop(s)' it up. He exhausts the fiddler and pours whiskey. In the upstairs room Eben is looking at the baby. Abbie goes upstairs and Cabot leaves for outside, 'fresh air', as she has told him not to 'tech' her. The guests gossip after he goes and we see Eben and Abbie upstairs and she professes her love for him,

> 'Don't git feelin' low. I love ye, Eben. Kiss me.'

Cabot says he's going to rest in the barn. The scene concludes with the fiddler playing in celebration of 'the old skunk gittin' fooled!'

Scene Two

Eben is outside half an hour later and Cabot is coming back from the barn. Cabot tells him to get a woman inside and he might get a farm. Eben replies that this farm's his and Cabot mocks him. He tells her Abbie has been promised the farm for her son and Eben is angered thinking Abbie has tricked him.

Eben goes to kill her but Cabot is too strong for him and Abbie comes out to stop him choking Eben. Cabot tells him he's weak and goes inside to celebrate. Abbie tries to be tender with Eben but he rejects her and calls her a liar.

> 'Ye're nothin' but a stinkin' passel o' lies. Ye've been lyin' t' me every word ye spoke, day an' night, since we fust – done it. Ye've kept sayin' ye loved me....'

She says she loves him and tells him that the promise was made before they fell in love. He says he'll go to California.

They argue and he 'torturedly' says he wished the baby had never been born. Abbie is distraught and she says she'd kill the baby to prove her love for him. He says he won't listen to her but she calls after him that she can 'prove' she loves him and she 'kin do one thin' God does'. Abbie is desperate at the end of the scene.

Scene Three

It is now just before dawn and Eben is in the kitchen ready to leave. Abbie is near the cradle with 'her face full of terror'. She sobs but Cabot stirs and she goes to the kitchen and flings her arms around Eben, kissing him 'wildly'. She says 'I killed him' and he thinks she means Cabot but is horrified when she tells him it's the baby.

Eben states it was his baby and she says she loved it but loves him more. He is angered,

> 'Don't ye tech me! Ye're pizzen! How could ye – t' murder a pore little critter – Ye must've swapped yer soul t' hell!

and tells her that he is getting the Sheriff and heads, 'panting and sobbing' to town. She calls out to him that she loves him.

Scene Four

It is after dawn and Abbie is in the kitchen. Cabot wakes in his room and is concerned that he has woken late. He checks the baby and is proud it is quiet and asleep. He goes down to Abbie in the kitchen and she tells him the baby is dead. He runs to check and comes back down and asks 'why?'

In a rage she tells him it was Eben's son and that she loves Eben, not him. He blinks back a tear and then gets 'stony' so he can carry on and says he is going to get the Sheriff. Abbie tells him that Eben's already gone so that Cabot tells her he'll 'git t' wuk.' He then tells her he'd never have told and now he's going to be 'lonesomer'n ever!' Eben comes back and Cabot tells him to get off the farm.

Eben asks for her forgiveness and tells her he loves her. He says he realised he loved her at the Sheriff's and they have a chance to run away but Abbie says she'll take her punishment. Eben says he will share it with her and plans to tell the Sheriff they planned it together. They think they can stand it together and then Cabot comes back.

He goes into a long tirade and tells them how he's let the stock go and will burn the house down. He too plans to go to California but finds that Eben has gotten to his money first. Cabot says that this is a sign from God to him to stay and that 'God's hard an' lonesome!' At this point the Sheriff comes and Eben says he was involved with the baby's murder.

Cabot says 'Take 'em both' and leaves to get his stock. The sun is coming up and as they are led away Eben says the farm's 'Purty' and Abbie agrees. The Sheriff finishes the play with the line, 'It's a jim-dandy farm, no denyin'. Wish I owned it!'

OTHER RELATED TEXTS

Fiction / Non-fiction / Drama

- *Wonder* – R G Palacio
- *First they Killed My Father* – Luong Ung
- *The Graveyard Book* – Neil Gaiman
- *Looking for Alaska* – John Green
- *Eleanor and Park* by Rainbow Rowell
- *The Fault in Our Stars* – John Green
- *We All Fall Down* – Robert Cormier
- *The Old Man and the Sea* – Ernest Hemingway
- *The Fire Eaters* – David Almond
- *Ender's Game* – Orson Scott Card
- *Hatchet* – Gary Paulsen
- *Inside Black Australia* – Kevin Gilbert
- *Sapiens: A Brief History of Humankind* – Yuval Noah Harari
- *Peeling the Onion* – Wendy Orr
- *Raw* – Scott Monk
- *Six Degrees of Separation* – John Guare
- *The Book Thief* – Markus Zusak
- *When Dogs Cry* – Markus Zusak
- *Holes* – Louis Sachar
- *The Outsiders* – S.E. Hinton
- *Roll of Thunder, Hear My Cry* – Mildred D. Taylor
- *A Small Free Kiss in the Dark* – Glenda Millard
- *Monster* – Walter Dean Myers
- *Lord of the Flies* – William Golding
- *Jandamarra* – Steve Hawke
- *A Separate Peace* – John Knowles
- *A Monster Calls* – Patrick Ness
- *The Pigman* – Paul Zindel
- *The Invention of Hugo Cabret* – Brian Selznik

- *Emerald City* – David Williamson
- *Silent Spring* – Rachel Carson

Films and Television

- *The Human Experience* – Charles Kinnane
- *My Brilliant Career* – Gillian Armstrong
- *Broadchurch* – James Strong & Euros Lyn
- *Twinsters* – Samantha Futerman and Ryan Miyamoto
- *Be My Brother* – Genevieve Clay - Smith
- *What's Eating Gilbert Grape* – Lasse Hallstrom
- *Pleasantville* – Gary Ross
- *Eternal Sunshine of the Spotless Mind* – Michel Gondry
- *Taxi Driver* – Martin Scorsese
- *Tootsie* – Sydney Pollack
- *Back in Time for Dinner* – Kim Maddever
- *The Godfather* – Francis Ford Coppola
- *Friends* – David Crane and Marta Kaufmann
- *Dawson's Creek* – Kevin Williamson
- *Orange is the New Black* – Jenji Kohan
- *Boy Meets World* – Michael Jacobs and April Kelly

Website – quote on literature and the human experience

*http://view2.fdu.edu/academics/university-college/school-of-humanities/
english-language-and-literature-program/*

At its most fundamental level literature explores what it means to be a human being in this world and tries to describe what our human experience is like. As such, literature pushes us to confront the large human questions that have plagued humankind for centuries: issues of fate and free will, issues relating to our role in the universe, our relationship to God, and our relationships with others. Studying literature not only helps us to understand the complexity of these questions intellectually, but because of its very nature, it allows us to experience these tensions vicariously. Literature does not just tell us about human experience; it recreates it in a way we can feel and visualise. In other words, it calls for a total response from us—it stretches us beyond who we are.

First, literature can enhance our ability to relate to people. Because literature focuses on human relationships and self perception, it can broaden our own experience—to help us understand different kinds of people, different cultures, different problems—and, consequently, help us better understand our own relationships with others.

The study of literature also helps to foster an appreciation for beauty, symmetry, and order. This means more than the intuitive response of liking or disliking something we see or read or hear; it means a carefully thought-through response that will enhance appreciation—not destroy it.

Perhaps the most important skills that the study of literature teaches are analytic and synthetic skills. In learning to read carefully and analytically, we learn to ask hard questions both of the work and of ourselves. And as we seek to discover the relationships between the ideas and images we uncover in a work, our ultimate goal is to see the whole—to see how the parts work together to make the piece what it is. In grappling with the complex and difficult ideas contained in literature, we learn to accept the multiple dimensions and ambiguity that are so often present in life.

Finally, the study of literature will also help develop our writing abilities as we come to value the written word and understand its power to communicate.

Beyond all of these skills, however, it is not what literature can do for us as individuals as much as what it can do to us. Literature speaks to the whole person. Listen to it, says C. S. Lewis, and you will be changed.

Poetry

- 'Warren Pryor' – Alden Nowlan
- 'The Gardener' – Louis MacNeice
- 'The Improvers' – Colin Thiele

Songs

- *Be My Escape* – Relient K
- *Mandolin Wind* – Rod Stewart
- *Roxanne* – The Police
- *Wake Me Up When September Ends* – Green Day
- *Under Pressure* – Queen & David Bowie
- *Candle in the Wind* – Elton John
- *Empire State of Mind* – Alicia Keys
- *Gold Digger* – Kanye West
- *We Are Young* – Fun.
- *Centrefold* – J. Geils Band
- *It's Time* – Imagine Dragons
- *We Cry* – The Script
- *If I Were a Boy* – Beyoncé
- *Shake it Out* – Florence + the Machine
- *C'mon* – Panic! At the Disco & Fun.
- *I Don't Love You* – My Chemical Romance
- *Sing* – My Chemical Romance
- *1985* – Bowling for Soup
- *What About Me* – Shannon Noll
- *Sinner* – Jeremy Loops
- *7 Years* – Lucas Graham

- *Bitter Sweet Symphony* – The Verve
- *Ghost!* – Kid Kudi
- *Good Riddance (Time of Your Life)* – Green Day
- *Expectations* – Belle and Sebastian
- *After Hours* – We Are Scientists
- *Write About Love* – Belle and Sebastian
- *Trust Your Stomach* – Marching Band
- *Heaven Knows I'm Miserable Now* – The Smiths